TRUTH, LIES & ALIBIS

Images and Words
by CHRISTINE KINSEY

This book is dedicated to my mother Gladys May Kinsey 1908-2005 and to all other women whose voices have not been heard.

Christine Kinsey in her studio

FFOTOGRAFF GAN / PHOTOGRAPH BY BERNARD MITCHELL ©

Morfudd 2 – *olew ar gynfas / oil on canvas 67 x 59 cm*

'It seems, then, that memory is less about an objective recall of facts, more a creative, personal and imaginative process of identity construction'.

ALISON WEBSTER *You Are Mine: Reflections on who we are* (London: SPCK, 2008).

First published in 2023 by the H'mm Foundation.

The H'mm Foundation, Grove Extension, Room 426, Swansea University, Singleton Park, SA2 8PP.

ISBN 978 1 9999522 5 9

A CIP catalogue record for this book is available from the British Library.

Cover painting – Gwylnos / Vigil (detail) *olew ar gynfas / oil on canvas 183 x 122 cm*

Design: Andy Dark
Typeset in Freight
Printed and bound by Gwasg Gomer, Llandysul, Ceredigion, Wales

www.thehmmfoundation.co.uk

Cynnwys | Contents

DID NOT
LEVEL
BE ON A
WOULD HAVE
MEASURED
WIDER
NO. NO.
NO.
BUT THE NEARNESS

Rhagair | Foreword

M. Wynn Thomas
Athro'r Saesneg, a Deilydd Cadair Emyr Humphreys sy'n cydnabod llên Saesneg Cymru, Prifysgol Abertawe
Professor of English, and Emyr Humphreys Professor of Welsh Writing in English, Swansea University

Ali Anwar
Cyfarwyddwr, Sefydliad H'mm
Director, The H'mm Foundation

Ganed a maged Christine Kinsey ym Mhont-y-moel, ac un ffordd o leoli ei gwaith yw drwy ei ystyried yn gynnyrch y ffin. Oherwydd y mae'n amlwg i'w dychymyg gael ei gyffroi'n gynnar gan brofiadau ffiniol. Deuoliaethau, cyfosodiadau, rhaniadau, a nifer o batrymau ffufiol a lliwgar eraill, dyna sy'n peri i'w gwaith ganu. Dro ar ôl tro croesir trothwy yn ei lluniau, ac os camwn y tu hwnt i'r ffrâm cawn ein hunain wyneb yn wyneb â therfyn ein hamgyffred. Y mae'r lluniau yn mynegi dirgelwch cyfrin, presenoldebau annelwig, ac ynddynt mae'r corff yn cael ei gyniwair gan yr ysbryd, a'r gorffennol yn fythol bresennol. Fe'n hagtoffir o'r awdur hynod hwnnw Arthur Machen, a oedd hefyd yn frodor y ffin. Mae'n cael ei adnabod bellach fel awdur y stori ysbryd ddylanwadol honno *The Angel of Mons*, y nofel hynod *The Great God Pan*, a'r hunangofiant rhyfedd *Far off Things*, lle mae Machen yn dwyn atgofion am ddylanwad ffurfiannol Twmp Barlwm arno, a'i ymwybyddiaeth gynnar ei fod yn byw mewn ardal a oedd yn llawn ysbrydion y gorffennol.

Ymhlith y dylanwadau ffurfiannol y mae Christine Kinsey yn sôn amdanynt y mae'r aristiaid Celtaidd anhysbys, meistri diwylliant cyfoethog Byzantium, prif arlunwyr Tuscany a Siena, a chewri modern megis David Jones. Y mae hefyd wedi cydnabod pwysigrwydd yr arlunydd Almeinig mawr Max Beckmann ac mae dau sylw ganddo megis wedi gosod cywair ei dychymyg. Yn y cyntaf, sonia Beckmann am fynegi'r anweledig drwy'r gweledig. Yr oedd yn arlunydd synhwyrus yn ogystal ag yn arlunydd ysbrydol, ac y mae'r wedd erotig ar beintiadau Christine Kinsey i'w gweld yn ei defnydd o liw – mae'r

Christine Kinsey and Ali Anwar

Christine Kinsey was born and raised in Pont-y- moel and one way in which we find ourselves understanding her is as a borderer – one whose imagination was stimulated very early by border experiences, border states, border conditions. In her recent work this seems very evident, in the multiplying of identities, the doublings and re-doublings, parallels, divisions and assorted other juxtapositions, of form and of colour, with which her work sings. Her paintings are paintings of the state of liminality – to enter them is in fact always to be halted at the threshold of understanding. And it is an air of mysterious inwardness, of haunting presences, of the mirage of solidity, of flesh everywhere ghosted by spirit, and of the past everywhere gnawing into the present, that her painting convey. We are reminded of the writings of her near-neighbour, so to speak, Arthur Machen. He is best remembered as the author of the *Angel of Mons*, *The Great God Pan* and that extraordinary autobiography *Far Off Things*, where he writes of the spells exerted on him by the mystic tump of Twm Barlwm, and of his growing up in a haunted and haunting region.

As deeply informing influences she acknowledge artists of many periods, from the early Celtic,

Yr Adwy 3 / The Gap 3 – *siarcol / pensil ar bapur / charcoal / pencil on paper 90 x 55 cm*

coch a ddefnyddir ganddi, er enghraifft, yn awgrymu berw'r gwaed ond hefyd y 'red shift' sy'n nodweddu rhyw realiti ysbrydol diflanedig sy megis yn ymbellhau oddi wrthom yn barhaus. Un arall o sylwadau cofiadwy Beckmann oedd mai dyfais ddynol oedd amser, ond mae palas y duwiau oedd gofod. Y mae gwaith Christine Kinsey megis yn estyn gwahoddiad i ni i gamu i mewn i'r palas hwnnw – y mae hyd yn oed y bwaoedd diwydiannol y mae'n eu cofio o'i phlentyndod yn rhesi gosgeiddig sy'n ardduno'r palas hwnnw. Yn ei gwaith y mae amser yn cael ei drin fel agwedd ar ofod, a gofod yn cael ei drin fel drws sy'n ein harwain i ddynfnderoedd ein hanes hen fel dynoliaeth.

I'r perwyl hwn y mae'n arfer techneg darluniadol sy'n debyg i'r hyn a alwyd gan rai o feirdd yr Unol Daleithiau yn 'deep images.' Delweddau yw'r rhain sy'n codi i'r amlwg o eigion y meddwl, delweddau na ellir eu trosi i iaith y rheswm a'r deall. Y mae'n un o'r artistiaid hynny y mae eu gwaith yn gwireddu sylw enwog W.B.Yeats, 'the truth cannot be known, it can only be symbolised.' Ond gellir hefyd synied am y palas hwn a adeiledir yn ei gwaith fel mangre sy'n bod 'between here and now,' i ddefnyddio ymadrodd awgrymog R. S. Thomas, bardd y mae'n arbennig o hoff o'i waith. Awgrymu y mae y gall celfyddyd fyw a bod mewn man cyfrin y tu hwnt i gategorïau arferol yr ymennydd. Fel y dywedodd y beirniad Americaidd mawr Helen Vendler wrth drafod gerddi darlun R. S. Thomas, 'the art-transaction of his picture-poems exists in the space between the reproduced (spatial) painting and the (temporal) commentary, and is located in the invisible intersection where the two art works illuminate each other'.

Y mae gan Christine Kinsey gyswllt yn barod â Sefydliad H'mm. Y gyfrol gyntaf I gyd a gyhoeddwyd gennym oedd *Encounters with R. S. Thomas*, ac fe'I lansiwyd gan Osi Rhys Osmond yn Oriel Plas Glyn-y-Weddw, mewn Arddongasfa yn 2014 y bu Christine

through the Byzantine and the masters of Tuscany and Siena to moderns such as David Jones. Another influence has been the great German painter, Max Beckmann who made two comments that we imagine as acting as tuning forks for Christine Kinsey's imagination. In the first, he claimed that painting consisted of 'rendering the invisible visible, through reality.' He was as sensual as he was metaphysical a painter, and the sensuality – and specifically the erotic – dimension of Christine Kinsey's work is often unmistakeable: her reds, for instance, can be at once startlingly blood-scarlet, almost embarrassing the sight with their naked boldness, and yet signify the 'red shift' of an endlessly receding 'other' reality. Beckmann also remarked that 'Time is a human invention, but space is the palace of the gods.' Christine Kinsey's work is an invitation to us to step into that palace – and she even turns the viaduct arches of her childhood memory into arcades of that grander structure. Her work shows us time re-viewed under the aspect of space, and space as a revelation of our existence in deep time. To this end she also employs what American poets of the post-war period called 'deep images' – that is images that are prior to, and deeper than, rational apprehension and that resist rational translation. She is one of those for whom the truth, as Yeats was fond of remarking, cannot be known; it can only be symbolised. Yet her palace may perhaps be even better defined as a place 'between here and now', to echo the title of a volume by R.S. Thomas, for whom art is neither spatial nor temporal but occupies a space outside of our categories. As the great American critic, Helen Vendler, has observed, 'the art-transaction of his picture-poems takes place in the space between the reproduced (spatial) painting and the (temporal) commentary, and is located in the invisible intersection where the two art works illuminate each other.'

Yr Adwy 4 / The Gap 4
– *siarcol / pensil ar bapur / charcoal / pencil on paper 90 x 55 cm*

Kinsey yn gyfrifol am ei threfnu. Fe wnaethom gydweithio'n agos â Christine hefyd pan yn llunio *HON 2022 Women Artists in Wales*. Hyhi a fu'n gyfrifol am olygu a chyd-lynu y gyfrol.

Y mae Christine Kinsey yn arlunydd sy'n arbennig o sensitif i hud a lledrith iaith. Yn hynny o beth, hwyrach ei bod yn nodweddiadol o artistiaid Cymry, am eu bod wedi eu meithrin mewn diwylliant lle y perchir y gair, ac mewn cymdeithas lle y mae dwyieithrwydd yn tynnu eu sylw yn naturiol at deithi geiriau. Fel yr awgrymwyd mewn man arall, gellir synied am yr iaith Gymraeg fel 'dark matter' ein cymdeithas arbennig ni. Er ei bod yn anweledig fel arfer, y mae bob amser ac ym mhob man yn ddirgel ddylanwadu – a hyd yn yn oed yn llywodraethu – ein defnydd o'r iaith Saesneg. Y mae ymateb Christine Kinsey i farddoniaeth R. S. Thomas yn crisialu'r profiad o dröedigaeth, a hynny mewn dau ystyr. Ar y naill law mae'n gydnabyddiaeth o'r modd yr ysgogwyd hi gan y datguddiadau y bu'r farddoniaeth yn fodd i'w profi, ac ar y llaw arall mae'n gyfaddefiad o'r her a geir yn ei waith i drosi'r iaith lafar i iaith delwedd a lliw a phatrwm, yr iaith y mae'r artist wrth gwrs yn arbenigo ynddi. Y mae wedi sôn, yn briodol iawn, am ddawn R. S. Thomas a amlygir yng ngrym ei ddelweddau '[to explore] the interface between the worldly and the spirit through the imagination, an essential function of artists in the evolution of the culture of an independent Wales.'

Y mae'n hen bryd i ni longyfarch Christine Kinsey yn wresog iawn ar ei gwaith unigryw, ac i wir werthfawrogi a dathlu ei dawn. Cafwyd ganddi gorff o waith sy'n ein galluogi, fel y dywedodd R. S. Thomas, 'to witness the extent/ of the spectrum and grow rich/ with looking.' Y mae'r gyfrol hon sy'n talu gwrogaeth iddi yn dathlu degfed pen-blwydd *Sefydliad H'mm*. Mae'n waith y bu hir ddisgwyl amdano, ac mae'n goron deilwng ar yrfa hir a disglair o wasanaeth diwylliannol i'n cenedl.

Christine Kinsey is not a stranger to *The H'mm Foundation*. In fact, the first book we published, *Encounters with R. S. Thomas*, was launched by Osi Rhys Osmond at the Oriel Plas Glyn-y-Weddw at an exhibition curated by Christine in January 2014 to celebrate the life and work of R.S. Thomas. We also worked very closely with Christine on the publication of *HON 2022 Women Artists in Wales*. She edited and coordinated the production of this volume.

She is an artist quite extraordinarily susceptible to the bewitchment of language – in a way perhaps deeply expressive of a Welsh sensibility, formed as it is within a culture of the word, and further sensitised to language as a medium by the co-existence within Wales of two languages that are so vividly contrasted in sensuous character and in forms of expression. As we have suggested elsewhere, Welsh may be regarded as the dark matter of the mental universe of Wales – largely invisible, yet omnipresent, existing enormous gravitational force on Anglophone culture. Christine Kinsey's painterly response to R.S. Thomas involves a conversion experience – not only in the sense of being seized by a revelation of the truth and importance of his vision but also in the sense of being inspired by that experience to the difficult task of converting that revelation from one medium, or 'language', to another. She speaks, very properly, of the importance to her of Thomas whose 'imagery explores the interface between the worldly and the spirit through the imagination, an essential function of artists in the evolution of the culture of an independent Wales.'

Christine Kinsey deserves to be congratulated on producing a body of paintings that enables us, as we view them, 'to witness', in R.S. Thomas's words, 'the extent/Of the spectrum and grow rich/With looking.' Published on the 10th anniversary of *The H'mm Foundation*, this volume as a tribute to her work over a lengthy career is long overdue, and richly deserved.

Cyflwyniad | Introduction

Menna Elfyn
Athro Emerita Prifysgol Cymru, y Drindod Dewi Sant Professor Emeritus,University of Wales, Trinity Saint David
Emerita Professor of Creative Writing, University of Wales Trinity Saint David

Christine Kinsey yw un o artistiaid mwyaf blaenllaw Cymru. Mae wedi cysegru'r rhan helaethaf o bum degawd i beintio a darlunio, ac, wrth wneud hynny, wedi goleuo byd lle'r oedd menywod yn arfer bodoli ar gyrion gweledigaeth. Mae ei phroses greadigol yn cynnwys ffilm a barddoniaeth, sy'n cyfoethogi ei chraffter artistig o ganmol y cyfraniad y mae menywod wedi'i wneud i gymdeithas a diwylliant Cymru.

Yn cael eu dwyn i gof y mae ei hatgofion cynnar o blentyndod ac o ddod i oed yng nghymoedd De-ddwyrain Cymru, atgofion sy'n ymgorffori, gyda dycnwch a gras, y menywod a oedd yn gynhalwyr eofn eu teuluoedd a'u cymuned, ac y mae eu bywydau, at ei gilydd, yn anghydnabyddedig. Maent yn wirioneddol ddyrchafedig yn ei gwaith, ac yn ymddangos yn eneidiau rhydd a chytûn, yn arallfydol yn ogystal â daearol. Maent yn gwrthsefyll diffiniadau hawdd gan eu bod yn herio hyd yn oed y syniad o farwoldeb ac yn preswylio mewn bydoedd eraill. Maent yn byw yn y cof, ymhell ar ôl edrych ar baentiadau Kinsey, ac, o'r herwydd, yn cofleidio byd sy'n dragwyddol bresennol.

Dyma lwybr ysbrydol taith fewnol yr artist tuag at ddynoliaeth trwy brofiadau menywod. Mae 'Gwybydd yr hyn sydd o flaen dy wyneb, a bydd yr hyn sy'n guddiedig oddi wrthyt yn cael ei ddatgelu' yn adnod o Efengyl Thomas (5). Does dim rhyfedd felly fod paentiadau Kinsey yn ein gwahodd i archwilio'r fenywaidd gysegredig i gael ymdeimlad o adnewyddiad. Mae pwy oeddent ac o le y daethant yn deillio o oleuni lle nad yw'r alegori chwedlonol o Sophia/Doethineb fel ymwybyddiaeth o ddynoliaeth yr hollfyd, fyth ymhell, na chwaith yr hyn rwy'n hoff o'i alw *Y Gorwel Anwel*.

Yn ei gwaith, gwelwn y cydbwysedd rhwng y trosgynnol a'r agos, myfyrio a gweithredu, corff ac enaid. Mae'r gwleidyddol yn wir yn bersonol, fel y mae hen ddywediad mudiad y menywod yn ei ddatgan. Yma, mae Kinsey yn parhau i fod yn driw i'r gred

Christine Kinsey is one of the foremost artists in Wales. She has dedicated the best part of five decades to painting and drawing, and in so doing has illuminated a world where women had previously existed on the periphery of vision. Her creative process includes film and poetry, which enriches her artistic acuity in extolling the contribution women have made to the society and culture of Wales.

Her early memories of childhood and of growing up in the valleys of south-east Wales, are recalled and embody, with grit and grace, the women who were the spirited upholders of family and community, and whose lives have been mostly unacknowledged. They are indeed elevated in her work and appear as both free spirited and kindred spirits, ethereal as well as earthly. They resist easy definitions as they challenge the very idea of mortality and inhabit other realms. They live on in the mind, long after viewing Kinsey's paintings, thus embracing a world that is eternally present.

This is the spiritual path of the artist's interior journey towards humanity through the experiences of women. 'Know what is in front of your face, and what is hidden from you will be disclosed' is a verse from the Gospel of Thomas (5). No wonder therefore that Kinsey's paintings invite us to explore the sacred feminine for a sense of renewal. Who they were and where they have come from emanate a light where the mythical allegory of Sophia/Wisdom as the consciousness of universal humanity, is never far away, neither is what I like to call *Y Gorwel Anwel*, 'the Unseen Horizon.'

We witness in her work the balance between the transcendent and imminent, contemplation and action, body and soul. The political is indeed personal, as proclaimed by the well-worn adage of the women's movement. Here Kinsey remains true to that belief, as the women in her world view are in

Yr Iau / The Younger – *olew ar gynfas / oil on canvas 102 x 76 cm*

honno gan fod y menywod yn ei bydolwg yn symud yn barhaus; hyd yn oed pan fyddant yn sefyll, neu'n eistedd, maent yn parhau yn gadarn, yn herfeiddiol, ac yn gwbl ymwybodol bod eu hurddas a'u hunaniaeth yn eu meddiant. Ar adegau maent yn ymddangos fel tystion, yn drist ac yn brudd, neu yn y cysgodion, rhwng colofnau a allai'n hawdd fod yn demlau, yn atgofion am ennyd o du mewn capeli, neu lwyn cysegredig cynnar. Mae strwythur cyfansoddiadol y paentiadau yn creu gofodau lle mae menywod yn dod yn oddrych yn hytrach nag yn wrthrych y ddelwedd, gan gollfarnu'r modd y mae menywod wedi cael eu portreadu yn hanesyddol. Mae yna lawer o fotiffau o ddrysau neu gynteddau; mae'r rhain yn caniatáu mynediad, yn ogystal â gadael i'r gwyliwr gwestiynu math arall o bresenoldeb. Mae'r menywod yn aml yn cydlynu â'i gilydd mewn rôl gefnogol neu'n dwyn tystiolaeth; maent yn aml yn dwyn negeseuon, neu'n arwain ei gilydd o un byd dychmygol i'r llall. Mae'r bwâu yn thema sy'n codi dro ar ôl tro, ac mae i ymddangosiad y traphontydd a oedd yn estyn dros gymoedd ei phlentyndod ymdeimlad sy'n argoelus. Maent hefyd yn ailymddangos ar ffurf symbolau, lle mae ei dychymyg wrth greu bydoedd eraill yn datblygu.

Wedi'r cyfan, mae Kinsey yn chwedleuwraig sy'n rhoi i'w goddrychau y dynged honno y cyfeiriodd Grace Paley ati pan ddywedodd fod 'pawb real neu ddyfeisiedig yn haeddu tynged agored bywyd.' Yn sicr, mae yna ymdeimlad o ddeialog rhyngddi hi a'i phwnc ym mhob un o'i phaentiadau wrth iddi gloddio'n ddyfnach ac yn ddyfnach, fesul haen, er mwyn cyrraedd y fan i greu eneidiau. Yn ei gwaith, mae'r ysbrydol yn datblygu i fod yn 'ymwybyddiaeth barhaus, yn weithred o gadw'r foment.' Gellir amgyffred ei bod wedi mabwysiadu *anamnesis* (atgofion) Simone Weil, 'cyfeiriad yr enaid tuag at rywbeth nad yw'r unigolyn yn ei adnabod ond yn un y gall gydnabod ei realiti.'

constant motion; even when they stand, or sit, they remain resolute, defiant and fully aware of owning their dignity and identity. They at times appear as witnesses, sad and sombre, or in the shadows, between columns which could easily be temples, fleeting reminiscences of chapel interiors, or an early sacred grove. The compositional structure of the paintings creates spaces where women become the subject rather than the object of the image, denouncing the way women have been portrayed historically. There are many motifs of doors or hallways which allow access as well as leaving the viewer to question another kind of presence. The women often cohere with one another in a supportive role or bear witness; they often bring messages or guide each other from one imagined world to another. The arches are a recurring theme, the viaducts that spanned the valleys of her childhood appear with a sense of foreboding. They also reoccur as symbols where her imagination in creating other worlds takes shape.

Kinsey is after all a storyteller who allows her subjects that destiny which Grace Paley alluded to when she said that 'everyone real or invented deserves the open destiny of life'. There is certainly in all her paintings a sense of dialogue between herself and her subject matter as she digs deeper and deeper, layer by layer, in order to reach at soul-making. In her work the spiritual evolves into a 'continuous consciousness, a preservation of the moment'. One can intuit that she has taken on Simone Weil's *anamnesis*, 'an orientation of the soul towards something which one does not know but whose reality one does acknowledge'.

Her method of working is indeed fascinating, with a single word awakening her to the possibility of her creation. '*Drysfa*', '*Dadeni*', '*Alltud*', '*Ailenedigaeth*', '*Dadlennu*', to note a few examples, all convey vividly the genesis of her 'naked thinking heart' (Donne).

Mae ei dull o weithio yn gyfareddol, gydag un gair yn ei deffro i bosibilrwydd ei chreadigaeth. Mae '*Drysfa*', '*Dadeni*', '*Alltud*', '*Ailenedigaeth*', '*Dadlennu*', i nodi rhai enghreifftiau, oll yn cyfleu tarddiad ei 'chalon noeth feddylgar' (Donne) i'r dim. Trwy'r un gair mae hi nid yn unig yn gallu 'gwybod' am ei phwnc ond hefyd ymgolli ynddo, fel ei bod yn datgelu'r gwahaniaeth hwnnw sydd yn y Gymraeg rhwng *gwybod* ac *adnabod*. Mae'n defnyddio'r holl syniad o *latai* (negesydd cariad) yn y *llateies* fenywaidd. Yn y fan hon, mae'n mabwysiadu'r ddyfais a ddefnyddiwyd gan Dafydd ap Gwilym a beirdd Cymraeg canoloesol eraill: sydd, wrth gynnig anrheg i anwylyd, yn moliannu'r negesydd, a allai fod yn wylan neu'r gwynt. Mae'r cerddi yn talu teyrnged i'r negesydd cyn dathlu ysblander yr anrheg neu ganmol y ferch dan sylw. Gellid dod i'r casgliad bod llateies Kinsey yn ymgorfforiad o'i safiad anhunanol, sef cynnig ei delweddau fel y posibilrwydd o olwg amgen ar y byd, ond gyda chariad bob amser yn sylfaen ganddi.

Ac eto, fel y mynnodd Joseph F. Graham, 'Nid yw geiriau yn disodli'r meddwl; maent yn meddiannu lle gwahanol', a gellid dweud yr un peth am waith Christine Kinsey. 'Rydym yn egni,' meddai wrthyf, wrth i ni drafod y llewyrch gweledigaethol yn ei phaentiadau sy'n atseinio'n ôl i eiliad mewn digwyddiad yn ystod plentyndod y mae ei ddwyster wedi aros gyda hi. Mae'r chwilio hwnnw am yr egni dwyfol mor fetaffisegol ag y mae'n real i artist y mae ei chelfyddyd yn cwmpasu byd a wnaed mewn modd dwfn a chymhleth.

Y cyfraniad mawr arall y mae Christine Kinsey wedi'i wneud i'r byd celf yng Nghymru yw trwy fod yn Gyd-sylfaenydd a Chyfarwyddwr Artistig Canolfan Gelfyddydau Chapter yng Nghaerdydd rhwng 1968 a 1976, a hynny ar y cyd â'i chydymaith gydol oes, yr artist Bryan Jones. Aethant ill dau ati, ar y cyd â'r awdur Mik Flood, i gynllunio a hyrwyddo

Through the single word she is able not only to 'know' her subject but immerse herself in it, so that she reveals that distinction in Welsh between *gwybod*, to know about things and *adnabod* to know a person. She reappropriates the whole idea of *llatai* (a love messenger) into the feminine *llateies*. Here she is adopting the device used by Dafydd ap Gwilym and other medieval Welsh poets: who, in offering a gift to a loved one, praise the messenger, which might be a seagull or the wind. The poems pay tribute to the messenger before celebrating the splendour of the gift or praising the girl in question. One could conclude that Kinsey's *llateies* epitomises her altruistic stance, offering her images as the possibility of an alternative view of the world, but with love always as her foundation.

Yet as Joseph F. Graham asserted 'Words do not take the place of thought, they occupy a different place', and the same could be said of Christine Kinsey's work. 'We are energy', she tells me, as we discuss the visionary gleam in her paintings which echoes back to a moment in a childhood incident that has remained with her in its intensity. That search for the divine energy is as metaphysical as it is real for an artist whose art encompasses a world made deep and complex.

The other great contribution Christine Kinsey has made to the art world in Wales is as Co-founder and Artistic Director of Chapter Arts Centre in Cardiff between 1968 and 1976 along with her lifelong companion, the artist Bryan Jones. They, together with the writer Mik Flood, planned and promoted events with the aim of setting up an art centre in Cardiff, for Wales. The move into a condemned school in Canton in 1970 turned their vision into a reality, making contemporary arts accessible to a wider audience. They recognised in those early days the need to develop spaces where creativity could foster in all disciplines and links could be forged

Llyfr lluniadu – Drawing book – Cyfres Ddawns / Dance Series – i / for Menna.

digwyddiadau ac iddynt y nod o sefydlu canolfan gelf yng Nghaerdydd ar gyfer Gymru. Roedd symud i ysgol gondemniedig yn Nhreganna yn 1970 wedi gwireddu eu gweledigaeth, gan wneud celfyddydau cyfoes yn hygyrch i gynulleidfa ehangach. Yn y dyddiau cynnar hynny, roeddent yn cydnabod yr angen i ddatblygu gofodau lle y gellid meithrin creadigrwydd ym mhob disgyblaeth a lle y gellid ffurfio cysylltiadau rhwng y gwahanol ffurfiau ar gelfyddyd. Mae eu breuddwyd o ysbryd creadigol ffyniannus yn sicr wedi cael ei chydnabod ledled y byd gan fod Chapter heddiw yn esiampl o arloesedd a ddylai gael ei hefelychu mewn oes o brynwriaeth faterol.

Mae rhywun yn meddwl tybed sut y cafodd y cyfuniad o'r gwahanol ffurfiau celfyddydol effaith ar y math o artist y byddai Christine Kinsey yn datblygu i fod; mewn gwirionedd, gellid yn hawdd ei hystyried yn un o'r cymeriadau niferus yn ei phaentiadau, yn dal gafael ar sylfeini'r gorffennol ond hefyd yn ymhyfrydu yn newydd-deb y presennol ac, fel erioed, yn ymgysylltu â chynulleidfa, gan ei meithrin a'i goleuo trwy ei hathrylith dawel.

Credaf y bydd y llyfr hwn yn plesio selogion a newydd-ddyfodiaid i'w gwaith, fel ei gilydd. Mae ei ehangder a'i ddyfnder yn sicr yn haeddu astudiaeth fanwl, oherwydd y tu ôl i'r cynfasau mae yna fywyd sy'n ymroddedig i beintio, ac artist sy'n haeddu cydnabyddiaeth fyd-eang. Mor ddiolchgar y dylem fod ei bod yn parhau i'n syfrdanu gyda'i gweledigaeth farddol unigryw. Dylem ni, genedl y Cymry, ddathlu'r ffaith ei bod, yn flaenaf oll, yn perthyn i ni, ond gan hefyd sylweddoli bod ei phaentiadau o fenywod yn cadarnhau ein bod ni oll yn rhan annatod wirioneddol o'r bydysawd rhyfeddol.

between the various art forms. Their dream of a creative spirit that would flourish has indeed been recognised worldwide, for Chapter today stands as a beacon of innovation that should be emulated in an age of materialistic consumerism.

One wonders how the fusion of the various art forms had an impact on the kind of artist Christine Kinsey was to become; in fact she could easily be seen as one of the many characters in her paintings, holding on to the foundations of the past while also relishing the newness of the present day and, as ever, engaging with an audience, nurturing, enlightening them with her quiet brilliance.

This book, I believe, will delight both enthusiasts and newcomers to her work. Its breadth and depth are certainly worthy of close study, for behind the canvasses is a life committed to painting and an artist who deserves worldwide recognition. How grateful we should be that she continues to dazzle us with her unique poetic vision. As a Welsh nation we should celebrate the fact that she belongs to us, first and foremost, while realising also that her paintings of women affirm that we are all indeed an integral part of the wondrous universe.

Alibis ***Looking both ways***

Born in a gap caught between two countries I look both ways into enfolding hills
Two languages meet stamp pathways cross run into each other
Industrial alchemy changed mines and quarries into tokens spent only in English
Welsh walks me to the edge wrapped in a woollen blanket cwtshed in fragile security
Exposed on each side words incised on stone and slate make good fences.

1

Rhyfel, Dogni, Llymder a'r Gwrth-ddiwylliant

War, Rationing, Austerity and the Counterculture

Blynddoedd Ffurfiannol

Formative Years

'And where do you think *you're* going?' a woman's voice rang out from the yard next door to our terraced house in Pont-y-moel, Monmouthshire. I quickened my steps along the garden path, went through the gate into the back lane and ran swiftly down the hill to the Patch, an area of grass with swings and a roundabout. The children I usually played with had gone on the annual Sunday School outing to the funfair at Barry Island on the south Wales coast. Unable to go, the day began as a great disappointment; but the sun was shining and I decided to walk up the mountain above the Patch. I passed the viaduct that straddled the valley between Cwm Fields and Cwmynyscoy, which had boarded up arches where we hid to play secret games as imaginary people in imaginary worlds. After crossing the bridge over the stream that flowed into Afon Lwyd, a steep climb led me onto the Twmp, part of the lower levels of Mynydd Maen which rose gradually to Twm Barlwm mountain. Lying amongst a haze of blue harebells and long grass, with the warm sun on my face and looking out across the valley, I felt for the first time, at the age of seven, the wonder of being alive.

Christine – Pont-y-moel infant school
second row / second from the left

The feeling of joy on the mountain was in sharp contrast to my experience of life at home. My father, David Edward Kinsey, died aged forty-five of cardiac failure in January 1949, when I was six. His death left our house pervaded with grief. I wasn't told he had died and at first thought he had been taken away to prison. Other thoughts stimulated recurring dreams of my father and me holding hands and walking through Pont-y-pool Park Estate wood yard, when suddenly, from behind, the felled tree trunks begin to roll towards us, faster and faster. We start to run, I let go of his hand and get away, but my father is run over by the massive tree trunks and is killed. For much of my childhood I felt guilty, believing his death was my fault. My mother was unable to talk about him for the rest of her life, and neither were other family members. Early memories of my father are of him being very strict and using corporal punishment; children were expected to be 'seen and not heard'. In the letter he wrote to a member of my family about disciplining me, he describes how my behaviour is improving by relating how many times he had 'smacked' me and then goes on to write that 'she still comes up for more, if it's guts that's needed, this child has it and some to spare'. Determined not to cry when being 'taught a lesson' I detached myself from the pain by watching an imaginary butterfly hovering in front of me, thinking how beautiful it was.

My father has been an elusive figure in my life, and so there has been a need to try and construct a person from photographs, documents and snippets of other information to piece together the missing years. He was born in 1903 in Pontnewynydd, Monmouthshire. His mother, Mary Lavender, died when he and his brother were teenagers and they continued to live with their father, Edward who was a collier, at Green Boat, near George Street, Pontnewynydd. Leaving school at the age of twelve, he seemed restless, working in a range of jobs in the South Wales Valleys, from a men's clothing store to a clerk at the steel sheet works. Being employed in the steel industry during the Second World War, he was exempt from the armed forces. It seems he liked to draw and had created a self-portrait, as well as being accomplished at sign-writing, but no examples of these had been kept. During the 1926 General Strike my father and his brother, as members of the choir Gwalia Gleemen of Pont-y-pool, which was the official miner's choir of the Clapham labour party, travelled to London and other areas of England in order to raise money and it send back to families affected by the Strike. This was one of the many Welsh choirs that travelled, often on foot, to venues both inside and outside Wales, raising money to send back to their communities. The two brothers became part of a quartet called the Four Dons that sang barbershop harmonies; they considered becoming professional, but one of the men was reluctant to be away from home. The Four Dons returned to Wales and continued to perform with the Gwalia Gleemen.

Merch gyda Barcud / Girl with a Kite – *gouache ar bapur / gouache on paper 84.1 x 59.4 cm*

My mother, Gladys May Charles, was born in 1908 and married my father in November 1932; I was born in October 1942 – a 'war baby'. The combination of the General Strike of 1926, the South Wales miners' strike of 1936 and the Second World War, which

Gwalia Gleemen of Pont-y-pool – my father front row – second from the left

The Four Dons – my father second from the left.

started in 1939, had a devastating effect on the community and took its toll on the health of adults and children alike. During the war and the following years, when food was rationed, the small amounts of butter, cheese, milk and meat allowed were given to my father, who had suffered ill health in the years before his death. Part of his staple diet was tripe cooked with onions in milk, which always seemed to be simmering on the stove, together with elderflower tea. During this time women would deprive themselves of food, even during pregnancy, unwittingly creating possible health problems for children in later life. In December 1948 my father's brother died and by the end of January 1949 we had lost my father. From that point on we had very little to do with his family.

I lived with my mother, a much older sister and my maternal grandmother, known as 'our Ma', who was deaf. She was born in 1870, the youngest of eleven children; our house was one of the four houses that had been built by my grandmother's bachelor brother. On his death, he left a house to my grandmother, as well as one to my mother, who lived in hers for 95 years, and one each to her sister and brother. My maternal grandfather was blind from his early fifties and worked as a basket weaver with the Blind Institute in Newport, Monmouthshire. Our house was one of the first in the road to have a 'bath-room', which was installed by the Blind Institute for my grandfather to soak wicker to make baskets; we took advantage of such a luxury and ousted the wicker for Friday bath nights. There were aunties who visited my mother and grandmother and our house was dominated by women after my father died. Whenever my mother said that I had grown out of clothes, there were aunties that provided hand-me-downs from older children; there were aunties who constantly told my mother how to 'bring me up', and one auntie who told me that everyone knew that I was evil because it showed on my face – I was troubled by teenage acne. The only man in the family at that time was an uncle who lived next door and worked as a sawyer at Tirpentwys Colliery. He returned home each evening carrying pieces of wood, choosing some to build a nesting

My mother – second from the left – with the 'aunties' in Ilfracombe

house and an aviary for beautiful, fragile, exotically coloured birds: budgerigars, canaries and African cut-throat finches. The nesting house was used to breed birds and the oppressive, stifling heat of the many lamps, a narrow passage between cages and feeling trapped, like the vulnerable captured birds, left an impression that continues to haunt me.

'Ma' – *gouache ar bapur / gouache on paper 84.1 x 59.4 cm*

My family and our neighbours shared recent memories of the Second World War and the aftermath of bombing raids on Swansea, when the sky was lit up by buildings on fire and seemingly endless nights spent in the cupboard under the stairs, or *cwtsh dan star*, as it is known in Welsh, wearing gas masks; a Mickey Mouse gas mask for children was kept in the *cwtsh dan star* long after the war ended. During those fearful nights the families listened to German Luftwaffe planes flying overhead locking for landmarks to direct them for bombing raids, not only on Birmingham, but also the Royal Ordnance Munitions Factory in Glascoed, between Pont-y-moel and Usk. The pro-German propaganda broadcasts on the radio were intended to terrify local people. Lord Haw-Haw, in his warnings about bombing the Glascoed factory would refer to the Folly Tower in Pont-y-pool Park as one of the landmarks. The tower had been built in the late eighteenth century by John Hanbury, a landowner and ironmaster, on his Pont-y-pool Estate. The Munitions Factory was heavily camouflaged and never bombed.

After my father died there was very little money coming into the house to support the family. The widow's pension was 10 shillings per week and family allowance 5 shillings. My mother, who had left school at twelve years of age, needed to find a job which was difficult for women in the Valleys. When the company British Nylon Spinners (BNS) built a factory at Mamhilad, between Pont-y-moel and Abergavenny which opened in 1948, it boasted the largest factory floor in Europe, and initially employed only men. In 1950, my mother was one of the first women to be employed on the same production line as the men, working in shifts burning nylon off spindles. Men and women were employed to do exactly the same work, but women were paid a fraction of what the men were paid and

Siwrnai / Journey 1-9 – *olew ar gynfas / oil on canvas 20.5 x 20.5 cm*

accused of taking men's jobs and working for 'pin money'. No consideration was given to the fact that my mother was supporting my teenage sister, my grandmother and myself. She was constantly exhausted, having to get up at 4 a.m. to arrive at work by 6 a.m. and getting home at 3 p.m. after the morning shift, and, if she was on the afternoon shift, starting at 2 p.m. and not arriving home until 11 o-clock at night. During my later childhood and teenage years, I looked after myself in the mornings and evenings on weekdays and did many household chores, including lighting fires and scrubbing the 'passage' between the stairs and front door, plus the front steps every Saturday morning, as well as tending to the needs of my grandmother who was bedridden for much of her later life. As a *treat* I was taken to an open day at the BNS factory; entering the area where my mother worked was like walking into hell. The noise was deafening, the smell putrid, the atmosphere cloying, and the heat overpowering. These were the conditions my mother worked in for fourteen years. At the age of ten, as a result of that visit, I was made very aware of the inequalities and prejudices women faced in their lives and this experience has been a major influence on the whole of my life and work.

Before my father died, in January 1949, I had been in hospital for various surgical operations and in October of that year tuberculosis was diagnosed in the glands that form part of the lymph nodes on the left side of my neck. It was not contagious but, because the condition was not well known at the time, it took four years of multiple confinements in Pont-y-pool and Panteg hospitals to treat and eventually remove the infected glands. During my first time in Pont-y-pool Hospital, parents were not allowed to visit their children. The ward was in the tower on the front of the building and I remember looking out of the window high up in the tower and seeing my mother walking away down the driveway. The nursing sister, in a starched white cap and apron and with a matching attitude, came into the ward to give me a teddy-bear-coloured dressing gown and an orange, which my mother had left at the door. During one of my stays in Panteg Hospital, I was put into a ward where the children were having eye operations and spent weeks in the dark with only red lights above each of the beds. The vision of a group of dark, ominous figures approaching my bed, lit only by the red lights, left me terrified. Being treated with penicillin for many months didn't solve the problem. The only solution was to surgically remove the infected tuberculosis nodes, leaving an ugly six-inch scar from behind my ear to under my chin. This scar was so unsightly it was not easy to live with as a young girl; some children saw it as a weakness and taunted me with the nickname 'scar face'. By the time I was twelve years old my mother persuaded the doctors to send me to the Skin Graft Unit at St

Siwrnai / Journey 10 – *olew ar gynfas / oil on canvas 20.5 x 20.5 cm*

Siwrnai / Journey 11 – *olew ar gynfas / oil on canvas 20.5 x 20.5 cm*

Lawrence Hospital, Chepstow, in an attempt to remove the scar. The operation was partially successful but throughout my teenage years and beyond, sometimes when talking to people they would not look straight at me but tilt their heads to one side to see the scar I was trying so hard to hide. Money was very scarce and my mother would not have been able to pay for any of the treatment or operations needed for my recovery. I would not have survived without the National Health Service, founded in 1948 by Aneurin Bevan, MP for Tredegar, Monmouthshire.

Having spent so much time in hospital, where no teaching was provided, my education suffered; the main memory I have of Pont-y-moel Infant and Junior School is of always trying to 'catch up' with lessons. I joined the infants' school aged four in September 1947 and the school's strict regime of reading, writing and learning arithmetic by rote was presided over by the headmistress, who insisted on complete silence in the classroom and in the corridors. Talking was not allowed, we always had to look to the front and sit up straight, and any deviation was punished by a rap on the knuckles with a ruler or a 'clout' to the back of the head. All the teachers were women and unmarried; at that time women teachers often lost their jobs when they married. We practised writing with a pencil and, progressing toward the junior school, at seven years of age, were introduced to writing with a nib-pen and ink from an inkwell. Splatters of ink on writing-books meant more raps with the ruler. The infants' and junior schools stood side by side, so going up to the 'big school' meant the same walk to school each morning: down the back lane to the Patch, under the viaduct, along the dram road (the disused railway line from the old quarry), through the Dingle and into the school yard. Education in the junior school was again dominated by the threat of corporal punishment, which was regularly administered to boys and girls alike. I clearly remember one occasion, when accused of turning to speak to the child next to me, being called to the front of the class and beaten across the legs. The teacher then accused me of trying to kick her, and sent me to the headmaster for a caning. Standing outside the door of his office, listening to whacks of the cane, a boy emerged with tears streaming down his face. Then it was my turn: three whacks on each hand. I refused to cry from the pain but my bruised and swollen hands were a reminder of the humiliation caused by the inherent cruelty in schools at that time.

The junior school curriculum was dominated by the tyranny of the eleven-plus examination. We were trained to answer quick-fire questions and the further children progressed through the school, the clearer it became as to who would pass the eleven-plus and who would fail. This became abundantly clear when I was ten and reached the examination class. There were four columns of double desks in the classroom; the children

Siwrnai / Journey 12-20 – *olew ar gynfas / oil on canvas 20.5 x 20.5 cm*

Siwrnai / Journey 21-23 *olew ar gynfas / oil on canvas 20.5 x 20.5 cm*

sitting in the column next to the window were given more attention and fitted the criteria to pass the tests. The further you sat away from the window, the more likely you were to fail. Having started in the column next to the window after returning from each stay in hospital, I was moved along the columns of desks to the one next to the door. As a result, in 1954 I failed the eleven-plus, much to the disappointment of my family.

The question was what should be done with me now: send me to Pont-y-pool Girls' Convent or Clark's Secretarial College in Newport? My mother wisely decided I would go to Wern Secondary Modern School in Sebastopol, a short bus ride away from Pont-y-moel. The school had a remarkable headmaster who recognised the ability of the children in his care and, although hampered by the national curriculum, attempted to devise a system that would give each child a broad education. He instilled in us the belief that, despite failing the eleven-plus, we were not failures and that we all had the potential to succeed in our ambitions. Wern Secondary Modern School was at the bottom of a hill in Sebastopol, between Pont-y-moel and Cwmbran. It was a single-storey building amongst terraced houses and was surrounded by a tarmac playground enclosed by a wire fence topped by barbed wire. The curriculum was divided into general science, arithmetic/mathematics and English language/literature, with all aspects of each subject combined in one lesson This was because the education authority assumed that we were incapable of retaining a broader understanding of individual subjects or learning another language. The history and culture of Wales were only acknowledged in the last few pages of a book on British history and the Welsh language was actively discouraged as being a waste of time, not only in the Wern but in secondary schools generally throughout Monmouthshire. We had art classes and painted with powder paint on sugar paper, usually the same painting for a whole term. The teacher was nicknamed Chalky, because if a boy or girl was caught talking, his aim with the chalk duster was extremely accurate. Consequently, he succeeded in stamping out my interest in the visual arts during my time in the Wern.

In 1955, after a period in hospital having plastic surgery on my tuberculosis scar, I returned to the Wern and began to feel, at last, there was some progress being made in my education. It was then that my success in sport was recognised, especially the long jump, and I qualified for the Monmouthshire games. To practise the jump, I started my run up outside the school entrance door, sprinted up the corridor, took off as my foot hit the wooden floor of the school hall and landed on a gym mat on top of coconut matting. The Monmouthshire games were held at Pont-y-pool County Girls' Grammar School on the top of Penygarn Hill. I had heard about the school, but I was unprepared for the location and grandeur of the building, which contrasted greatly with the Wern. The event was held on a sports field which included tennis courts, a hockey pitch, lacrosse field and a sandpit. My jump broke the Monmouthshire record, but the sports teacher at the Grammar School objected to this being allowed, because, she said, the wind was behind me. This experience reinforced my awareness of the huge difference between passing or failing the eleven-plus.

During my time in the Wern my mother continued to work at the BNS factory and she formed a friendship with a man who was homosexual; he became a very kind friend to me during my teenage years. At the time he was charged with having a sexual relationship with another man and there was a court case pending against him. He would visit us regularly, mostly for Sunday tea, and would stay to help me with my homework. We had three adult books in our house, on a shelf underneath the radio: the Bible, a medical dictionary and *Twilight of the Gods* by Richard Garnett. Our friend helped my mother buy me a set of *Encyclopaedia Britannica* as a Christmas present and several times he took us on holiday to Weymouth where we always stayed at the same guest house, with a couple who had two children. The father often went night fishing and, going into the bathroom in the morning, it was not unusual to find the bath alive with writhing eels awaiting their fate. I have photographs from these holidays showing my mother and me, but there isn't a single one of our friend. Some members of the family were outraged by our friendship with him; there were many arguments and we were ostracised, but my mother with her quiet strength and determination, did not pay any attention to the criticism. The court case against our friend in the 1950s did not materialise, although a distant relative, who lived locally, was found guilty, at nineteen years of age, of having a male homosexual relationship and was imprisoned for eighteen months. This was treated as a dark secret by the members of my family and never discussed. Homosexuality would be partially decriminalised in 1967, following the efforts of Leo Abse, our local MP for Pont-y-pool and then Torfaen, in the wake of the recommendations of the Wolfenden Report of 1957.

The headmaster at the Wern, together with other secondary school headmasters in Monmouthshire, devised a fifteen-plus examination in 1958 called the Monmouthshire Certificate of Education (MCE), which became the

Siwrnai / Journey 24 – *olew ar gynfas / oil on canvas 20.5 x 20.5 cm*

Certificate of Secondary Education (CSE). This was not fully introduced into the educational system in Wales until 1965. Previously, the majority of secondary modern pupils left school without any qualifications until the raising of the school leaving age to sixteen. In the Wern we were promised that if we passed 10 subjects in the MCE, we would be able to go on to a grammar school to sit O levels (the precursor of GCSEs). I passed nine subjects, but I failed cookery. Although agreeing that the cabbage in the bottom of my saucepan looked more like seaweed, I could not accept that this was a good enough reason to prevent me continuing my education, especially as I had missed so much school and I was only just beginning to 'catch up'. Leaving school at the age of sixteen, the only option would have been to go into one to the many factories to work, as I did not have the qualifications to get one of the sought-after jobs that offered training programmes. My mother could certainly have used the extra money, but she supported me when I said I was going back to the Wern to sit outside the door of the headmaster's office until he persuaded the headmaster of Abersychan Grammar School to allow me to transfer to his school. After weeks of determined waiting and not taking no for an answer, I was, at last, transferred. This meant buying a new school uniform, so my mother borrowed money from the Provident, paying it back at sixpence a week to the man who called at the house every Friday. The alternative was to buy from the tallyman on the 'never-never', which often meant the salesman tried to make sure you continued to buy from him, so that you were never out of debt.

My mother Gladys May Kinsey

During the two years between 1958 and 1960 I spent in school at Abersychan, I became angry, frustrated and very rebellious, recognising how the long absences from previous schools caused by my illnesses, together with the limited curriculum at the Wern, had restricted my education. I knew at that point I needed to find a way of channelling my feelings in a positive direction. Then I found the art room which became my sanctuary, spending most of my time there. It was over the town library, separate from the main school. The teacher, Evelyn Brierley, who was an artist in her own right, encouraged the group of five students, both male and female, to apply to Newport College of Art. I applied and was accepted. There were members of my family who tried to prevent me from going, saying that I was not good enough, as they knew students going to teacher training college who were much better than me, and I would just make fool of myself. My resolve to go to art college, with the support of my mother, was also motivated by a secret I had kept about myself since I was ten years old and which I had decided, up to then, would be better kept to myself.

Drawing book, Newport College of Art – Iard Gefn / Back Yard, Pont-y-moel – *inc ar bapur / ink on paper*

Newport and Monmouthshire College of Art, with its green copper dome, was a landmark building on the banks of the river Usk near the Severn estuary in Newport. It had been built as Newport Technical Institute in 1910 and was an art college from 1958 until 1975. The Edwardian marble entrance hall's sweeping staircase led up to a hierarchy of floors which accommodated students studying a range of visual disciplines. The top floor housed Fine Art in the Antique Room, a corridor lined with plaster casts of figures from antiquity, and the Life Room, under the green dome, where the human form was studied through drawing and painting. The College attracted students mainly from the eastern valleys of south Wales, who were supported by local authority grants to study the four-year course for the National Diploma in Design (NDD). The grants were crucial in enabling the students – who were mainly from working-class backgrounds – to attend the course, which I began in 1960. During my first two years, we followed a general course in art and design which included drawing from the figure; sculpture; ceramics; architectural and technical drawing; calligraphy; printmaking; and the textile arts. In my third year, I chose to specialise in painting, although I was not encouraged to do so by the tutors, because the design pathway was deemed more suitable for women. There were no women teaching in the Fine Art department and the limited Art History course did not include any women artists. Newport College of Art had built up a substantial reputation for fine art, especially painting, under the tutelage of the painter Tom Rathmell, who had trained in London at the Academy Schools. These Schools are part of the Royal Academy of Arts, with a lineage going back to the drawing and painting process that had been taught in the French Academy. We were encouraged to paint and draw our immediate environment; as most of the students came from coal-mining areas, this became one of our main subjects. It was a monochromatic world which also reflected the clothes we wore in this beatnik era; influenced by contemporary black-and-white French films, we favoured dark colours, and the paintings of Josef Herman were reflected in the way students portrayed their environment in colour and composition. Typical subjects were miners walking up a hill, with their backs to the viewer, strategically placed

Drawing book, Newport College of Art – Hunan Bortread / Self Portrait – *pensil ar bapur / pencil on paper*

Bryan and Christine
– Trafalgar Square, London 1963

telegraph poles on the right and left of the picture, and telegraph wires heading into a distant landscape with pit wheels and terraced houses.

It was during this time at Newport College of I met Bryan Jones, who would become my lifelong companion. He was older than most of the other students because, before enrolling in Newport, he had been one of the last men to be conscripted for National Service. Bryan gave me the greatest gift I could have received: he taught me not to just *look* but how to *see* and showed me there was a visual language I could learn which would give me a greater freedom to be able to develop my ideas. He also supported the way I worked, outside the accepted norm of what was deemed to be 'good drawing', and introduced me to literature, including poetry, and an intellectual and questioning approach to making art.

During my second year in art college, my mother met a man in the BNS factory and they decided they would marry. This was a surprise because I hadn't met him. At the time I was staying four nights a week in a shared room in Newport, unable to travel home after the evening classes we were expected to attend. Returning home one Friday evening, I was told all my things had been put into tea chests in the coal shed and I should take them away as soon as possible. This was a problem for me because I had nowhere to take them. The solution was found, with the help of a fellow student who had the use of a van, and the head of Sculpture who allowed me to store them in the cellar of the old school being used as the Sculpture department, in the Pill area of Newport. There they stayed for the next two years, while I continued to live in rented accommodation. I was never welcome in what I still considered to be my family home again. I was told after he died that before meeting and marrying my mother, he had a history of mental illness, which was kept a secret from her: he had been sectioned twice under the Mental Health Act and had spent time in Pen-y-Fal, a local hospital for mentally unwell patients. I was also told of a violent episode, when he attempted to attack a manager while he was working in BNS. As a bachelor, he lived in an acrimonious relationship with his family, including a sister and brother-in-law, with whom he shared a house. He transferred his previous obsessions with his brother and mother, after they had died, onto my mother and tried to exclude everyone else from her life. At the time, having a mental disorder or a person in the family with psychological problems was something to be ashamed of and so it was kept secret and not discussed, which meant he did not have the help he needed to manage his mental illness. Over the years my mother coped remarkably well with his obsessive behaviour, although there came a point when he bullied her into silence by his incessant repetitive talking and his aggressive insistence on a very regimented lifestyle. There were many times when I was concerned about leaving my mother in the house with him, but she insisted on staying in the house she had grown up in. We continued to keep in very close contact with each other, even though, at times, it was extremely difficult to find ways of talking and spending time together.

In my third year of the NDD in Newport, and beginning to specialise in Fine Art Painting, was when I met Elizabeth (Betty) Rathmell, a fourth-year student who introduced me to the paintings of Gwen John, whom she was writing about for her final-year essay. I became aware, for the first time, of a woman artist and that an internationally known Welsh woman painter had existed. Betty was one of the few women on the fine art course and the only woman from Newport to be accepted on the painting course at the Royal College of Art, London during the 1960s. Women who had elected to follow fine art courses were not usually taken seriously, and those who married other artists mostly let their husbands' careers, as artists, take priority. There are many women's accounts of being told there was to be only one artist, musician, writer, film-maker in the family and that would be the man. This was Betty's experience after she married Ian Drury in 1967. Like her, he was a student at the Royal College of Art; he was also the lead singer of the rock band The Blockheads. The film about him, *Sex & Drugs & Rock & Roll*, shows how the creativity of a very talented woman artist like Betty could be stifled by the egotism of their husband. Betty's premature death in 1994, aged fifty-two, was a major loss to family and friends, as well as the culture of Wales. During my student days, there was very strong social pressure for women to marry and have children; perhaps research into the lives and experiences of artists' wives would give us an insight into why there are so few known women artists from my generation still practising professionally. Not surprisingly, when women artists began to represent themselves, a significant number chose not to work in the male-dominated field of painting but looked for other ways of making art through a range of different media, encouraged by the transition from Modernism to Postmodernism.

Stories told through painting, performance, literature, photography and film about the experience of coming from the South Wales Valleys continue to reflect, in the main, a male perspective. Drawing and painting my external environment did not interest me as a student, and from the beginning of the third year of the NDD we were able to choose our own subject matter. Russian icon paintings were the first images to influence my work. The narrative represented by the figures and the signs and symbols which imbued the images with aspects of the female divine fascinated me, and continues to be a major

Yn null Sassetta / After Sassetta – *olew ar gynfas / oil on canvas 41 x 31cm*

Bryan – Hunan Bortread / Self Portrait – *gouache ar bapur / gouache on paper 20 x 40 cm*

influence on my work. In the first and only group discussion with a visiting lecturer, I was told that my painting of two girls in striped stockings sitting on a bench facing each other, which had been influenced by the medieval artist Andrei Rublyov's well-known painting of the *Trinity*, showed that I 'was trying to run before I could walk'. Such dismissive comments were typical and over the years I was often told by other male artists that 'all you do is bang on about women' and that I should not write that my paintings were about growing up *female* in the South Wales Valleys, because it would deter galleries from showing my work. Such comments did not dissuade me, and I did what I have always done: use men as a sounding board while saying to myself 'Well, if this is what men think, what do I think?' which has made me even more determined to follow my own path. At college we were discouraged from writing about and discussing authors, or developing our own ideas, and told that we should 'do our thinking and talking with the paintbrush'. The relationship between the word and the image was just beginning to emerge as an important aspect of my work and I became fascinated by the author, playwright and artist August Strindberg, who often drew on his personal experiences. In his biographical novel Inferno and his later plays *A Dream Play*, *The Ghost Sonata* and *To Damascus*, he writes about himself in a world from which he felt alienated. I recognised that his persona, imagery and writing were often misogynistic, but the transformative interior and psychological journey that he had taken through images and words helped to indicate the journey I wanted to take through my art.

At the age of seventeen my *secret* was at the centre of my interior life. In a coffee bar in Newport, a fellow student had been regaling me with stories about his grandmother who lived in Merthyr Tydfil and was a spiritualist and held seances. I hadn't heard anyone speak of these things before and decided to tell him my secret. Explaining that between the age of eight and ten years old I was drawn, for some time each day, to stand at a bedroom window at the back of our family's terraced house in Pont-y-moel and look out between the side walls of the house across a narrow valley to the lower slopes of Mynydd Maen. For over a year I was compelled to stand, watch and wait. On a day in March, a column of light appeared from one of the empty levels cut into the Twmp for pigeon cots. The light enclosed what can only be described as a *presence*, it grew upwards until it touched the clear blue sky and disappeared. The waiting was over, I had no need to go to the window again. I told him the *appearance* did not surprise me, but what did surprise me was that the intense need to go to the window had disappeared. He said it wasn't the kind of spiritualism his grandmother practised and didn't think she would be able to help me. The *appearance* is as clear to me today as it was. then, being held in that moment I experienced a *glimpse of true reality* which had nothing to do with the deities or dogma of any religion, it gave me an insight into another reality, impossible to understand through logic or reason. I didn't speak about my experience again for twenty-five years, but as part of my first exhibition of drawings and paintings I was determined to find a language to begin to explore the realisation that what we see and feel in the material world is not the totality of what it is to be human. The experience for me was a spiritual awakening and an awareness that we are made of the matter which makes up the universe and we are connected and belong to the whole of creation. It is the single most important experience of my life and I knew that this would be a defining factor in the way my creativity developed.

Throughout the 1960s a cultural revolution was taking place in art schools as education was being influenced by the emergence of Postmodernism. Although American non-figurative painting had started to influence some students in Newport, another major change occurred with an awareness of British Pop Art. The work of Peter Blake was featured in the first edition of *The Sunday Times* colour section on 4th February 1962, followed on 1st July that year by the *Art Student* cover, which showed a photograph of a woman art student working in her studio. Both these gave prominence to the emerging new visual art scene, as did the television programme *Pop Goes the Easel,* made by Ken Russell in the same year. This programme featured Peter Blake and included British Pop artists Peter Phillips, Derek Boshier and one-woman artist, Pauline Boty. Meanwhile, the NDD course in Newport was being replaced by the Diploma in Art and Design; this change led to the staff losing interest in teaching the NDD students, particularly in the life drawing classes. For me, however, this was more than compensated for by learning from fellow students and it gave me more time and freedom to pursue my own creativity. The final examination, after four years of study, in 1964 included a life painting and a three-figure composition; I was unable to complete the life painting and consequently failed the NDD, as I had developed Graves' disease, which is caused by an over-active thyroid gland. This illness had, in fact, completely overshadowed my time at Newport College of Art, because once again I needed to spend long periods of time in Pont-y-pool Hospital.

Edrych y ddwy ffordd 1-3 / Looking both ways 1-3 – *pastel / siarcol ar bapur / pastel / charcoal on paper 30 x 15 cm*

Bryan and I had planned to move to London at the end of the NDD course, and the expectation was we would get married, which we did in the small church of Llanfihangel Pont-y-moel on 1st July 1964. After the wedding ceremony we caught the train to London. We hadn't booked accommodation, but eventually we found a basement room in Paddington and decided to go to see the Ingmar Bergman film *The Silence*. Bryan and I would have preferred not to have married but it would have been a stigma on the reputations of our mothers, when they explained to family and friends that we had moved away together and were, so called, 'living in sin'. We had very little money but managed to rent a flat in Hornsey and Bryan found a job as a caretaker of a synagogue; we were extremely grateful to be allowed to feast on the pastries left over after various events in the Jewish calendar. I enrolled onto the life painting course at Hornsey College of Arts and Crafts in October the same year to complete the NDD, but because of student protests at the building in Crouch End, painting, drawing, 3D, crafts and printmaking were housed at Alexandra Palace. All subjects were taught in a huge hall, which had been the ballroom, making it look like a shanty town with students 'elbowing' space for themselves to work as the hall also housed the canteen, which was next to the life drawing area – it was like trying to work in the middle of a busy market place. I completely empathised with and supported the student grievances and the action that was being taken, but realising that I was not in a position to contribute to the student uprising and with the lack of facilities and no tutors, Bryan and I returned to Wales, and I completed my NDD at Newport in 1965. Hornsey College of Art was central to the student revolution by 1968, and this led to the occupation of the building in Crouch End for six weeks and a six-month lock-out, when departments were closed, tutors exiled and student activists expelled.

Meanwhile, Newport College of Art had moved away from traditional painting and sculpture courses when Conceptual and Interactive Arts became the main areas of study.

Edrych y ddwy ffordd 4 / Looking both ways 4 – *pastel /siarcol ar bapur / pastel /charcoal on paper 30 x 15 cm*

The precept of 'do your thinking and talking with your paintbrush' changed radically and in many creative areas presenting written concepts and talking about them seemed to be considered more important than making visual images. Changes also spread to Cardiff College of Art during the 1960s. When a Basic Design Course inspired by the theoretical writing in Herbert Read's *Education through Art* and the German Bauhaus with the premise that 'form follows function' was introduced into the Foundation Course it became one of the most radical art and design foundation courses in Britain. As a student on the Art Teacher's Diploma Course in Cardiff and supporting students who had enrolled on the Foundation course in Cardiff Art College, I realised the one thing that hadn't changed was the attitude toward women students and staff. In my experience, these courses continued to follow the strong male gender bias dictated by Bauhaus founder Walter Gropius, who said he believed men thought in three dimensions and women could only think in two. Women, therefore, were advised to follow courses in the textile arts and crafts, rather than painting, carving and architecture, consequently many women gave up their aspirations of becoming professional fine artists, which replicated my experience as a student in Newport College of Art and enforced my belief that this situation continued to put women at a great disadvantage because we were still attempting to be 'what we cannot see'.

The 1960s was a period of great change and the arts showed a way society could move forward after restrictions caused by the Second World War and its repercussions throughout the 1950s. The Swinging Sixties was the era identified with young people demanding more sexual and social freedom, it was a time when people who had lacked the opportunity to voice an opinion found a way to speak out and change their communities; practitioners in all the arts contributed to making these changes happen. Small touring agitprop theatre companies produced highly politicised work to support many of the grievances felt by the most vulnerable people in society, and film-makers and video artists exposed the injustices that working people were suffering. Some visual artists were no longer willing to support the dominant commercial gallery system and embraced the opportunity to expand their creative language by making work that was not 'saleable', often integrating painting, sculpture, performance, sound, film and video. Bryan, who had also been a student on the Art Teacher's Diploma course, and I often talked about the lack of venues in Cardiff, and in Wales in general, where these new art forms could be shown in public spaces. Our intention to make these art forms available to a wider audience propelled us into an extraordinary *chapter* in our lives.

Ymwacâd / Chi Rho – *olew ar gynfas / oil on canvas 102 x 77 cm*

Alibis ***In transit***

Arriving they looked for signs to reveal the way as their eyes grew accustomed to the light
words emerged names in a man-made language taking a name they left
a girl remained trying on the names one by one virgin servant whore Mary Martha
Magdalene would not fit unnamed in silence she portrayed the gap in the artist's eye.

2

Gweithredu Diwylliannol Radical a'r Gymuned

Radical Cultural Activism and the Community

Blynyddoedd Cynnar

Chapter Arts Centre, Cardiff – Early Years

Bryan and I first met Mik Flood, by chance, in December 1968. We had been renting a room in our house to students and when they went home for Christmas, he moved in. Mik had come to Cardiff from north Wales and initially worked in the steelworks, with plans to become a freelance writer. He was nineteen and Bryan and I were in our twenties and we were interested in the counterculture that had developed throughout the 1960s. Bryan and I as artists were also very conscious of the lack of venues for the contemporary arts in Wales, and the three of us began to discuss over the Christmas of 1968 what could be done to improve the situation. The National Museum of Wales in Cardiff occasionally showed contemporary art, some of it Welsh. The two private galleries in the city, the Howard Roberts Gallery and the Albany Gallery, had limited space. The New Theatre had housed the Welsh National Opera since 1954 and presented a wide variety of other productions, and the Casson Studio Theatre in Ruby Street hosted performances by amateur groups.

The most exciting area in Cardiff, for Bryan and I, was Butetown which had a long-established live music scene, with jazz played by highly accomplished local musicians. John

Co-founders and first Artistic Directors, Chapter Arts Centre, Cardiff. (Standing) Bryan Jones (Seated) left Mik Flood / right Christine Kinsey

Silva and his Quartet played in the wonderful Ghana Club, which was the front room in a terraced house which opened onto Bute Street and was owned by his mother-in-law. He arranged for international jazz musicians who were playing at Ronnie Scott's Jazz Club in London to come to the Ghana Club as part of their tours. The lively jazz scene also included pubs such as the Paddle Steamer and the Quebec, where Vic Parker, who played guitar and sang, was the resident musician. The shocking demolition of large areas of Butetown in the 1960s devastated the community and the cultural life, leaving Cardiff bereft of a very important part of its identity; one of the reasons Bryan and I wanted to set up a centre for the arts was to re-establish the music scene that had existed in Butetown. The remarkable Globe Cinema in Roath showed a season of continental avant-garde films each year, influencing a generation of artists, but was always under the threat of closure. There was also an absence of affordable studios, galleries, cinemas, and performance spaces to make and show the radical work that had been developing in the 1960s, so we decided to plan a way to fulfil these needs.

Over the kitchen table in our house in Pen-y-lan, during December 1968, we discussed a way forward and decided to form the Art Centre Project Group. Our aim was to publicise and raise enough money to set up an art centre in Cardiff and our first decision was to advertise the group in the *International Times* (IT), an underground magazine/newspaper which had been founded in 1966 and covered politics, the arts and the counterculture in Britain. It was one of the first of its kind to recognise the spread of a socio-cultural revolution dubbed the Swinging Sixties, with its hippy generation and flower power, including its slogans of free love and peace. Our advertisement invited anyone who was interested in setting up an art centre to join us. The only answer we received, which proved to be crucial, was from Peter Jones, the Art Director in the Welsh Arts Council which had been created in 1946, as part of the Arts Council of Great Britain, the organisation became independently established as the Arts Council of Wales in 1994. There had been a great deal of criticism about the pace of development relating to all the arts in Wales by the Arts Council of Great Britain in its annual reports. The 1971/72 report states that 'It is a common cry at present that Wales is stirring and re-gaining its old confidence and self-esteem. It is reasonable to expect this renewed national pride will demonstrate itself in artistic expression'. The report continues: 'Welshmen [sic] with an appetite for the arts must indicate very soon what they want and how they propose to pay for it. It is not for the Welsh Arts Council to say what they should or shall not have.' These comments showed how the Arts Council of Great Britain was ill-informed about the innovative avant-garde developments in the visual arts that had been taking place in Wales, led by Peter Jones during the 1960s and early 1970s. For the cultural life of Wales to develop there needed to be people within the Welsh Arts Council, regional arts associations and local authorities with the vision to support initiatives and new ideas, in addition to acknowledging Wales as a separate country and culture requiring a different policy.

Postmodernism had been gaining momentum during the 1960s in response to the Modernist era. Peter Jones perceived his work with the Welsh Arts Council as being creative as well as administrative he supported Postmodernist visual art in Wales, which was comparable to what was being produced anywhere else in Britain, some of which he knew would be very controversial. In the late 1960s, for example, he commissioned artists to create images that were enlarged and shown on advertising billboards, and large non-figurative sculpture in public spaces. Gordon Redfern, the architect of Cwmbran New Town, suggested to the Welsh Arts Council an exhibition based on the theme of art and society. It was the enthusiasm and expertise of Peter Jones that played a major role in supporting and creating the ground-breaking and contentious series of four exhibitions called *Art and Society*, the first three exhibitions were shown in major venues both in Wales and England. The first was *War* (1969) which was followed by *Work* (1970) and *Worship* (1971). *Sex* (1972) was the fourth exhibition and was particularly controversial, with complaints from schools and churches, the images were not fully displayed although the book Sex to accompany the exhibition was published and eventually some of the material was incorporated into the *Love and Marriage* exhibition. Ken Baynes was commissioned by WAC to curate the exhibitions which included graphics, cartoons, photographs, prints, films, painting, sculpture and performance from a broad range of cultures, as well as a comprehensive book to accompany each exhibition. The books were also written, compiled and designed by Ken Baynes, with contributions by Kate Baynes and Alan Robinson and the book *Art in Society* was developed from the four *Art and Society* books and were all published by Lund Humphries. Ken Baynes acknowledges in *Art in Society*[1] that

Book covers War / Work / Worship / Sex © Krysia Baynes

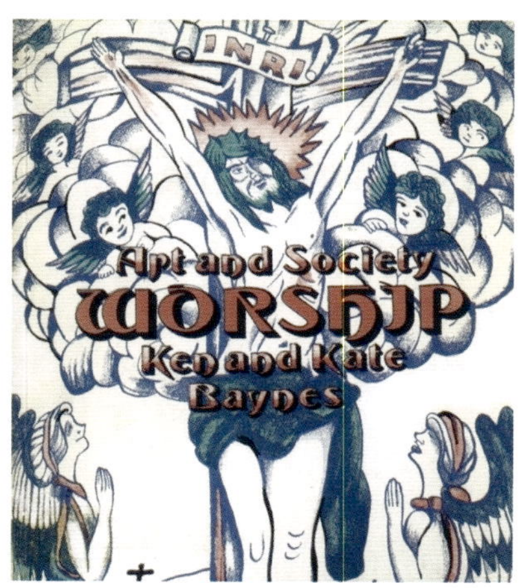

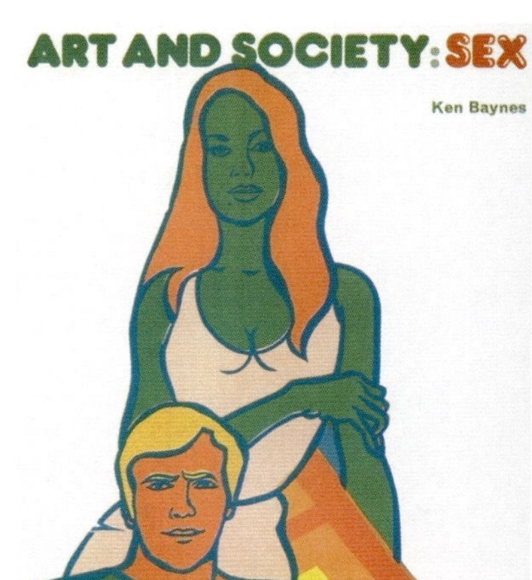

Peter Jones should be credited as co-author 'The ideas and approaches presented here have all been developed jointly with him. They spring from six years of the most fruitful discussion and debate that I have ever experienced. I have developed the greatest respect for his wisdom and for his subtle appreciation of the positive role which art can play in the development of human societies. Without his contribution, it simply would not have been possible to organize the exhibitions and write the book'. Peter Jones continued to support Postmodernist work; in 1968 Brian Lane staged a three-day event in Aberystwyth called *Fluxconcert by and for Fluxus*, which included musical scores by George Maciunas and George Brecht and in the National Eisteddfod in Wrexham in 1977 he initiated a performance art event in the visual art pavilion which included artists Joseph Beuys and Mario Mertz. This was the most radical development to date, causing negative repercussions, there were accusations of wasting public money and questions asked in the House of Commons. As a general protest against the lack of recognition, support and formal status of the Welsh language, Welsh artist and language activist Paul Davies performed *Welsh Not* on the Eisteddfod field.

Peter Jones' vision for the development of the arts in Wales went far beyond his remit as Art Director. His aim was that Wales should take a leading role in the international Postmodernist movements. He succeeded in offering artists from Wales, who worked in both the Welsh and English languages, the opportunity to develop their ideas in relation to the culture of Wales within an international context. He made all forms of the arts available to a wider audience, leaving a lasting legacy from which we still benefit today. His support was crucial to us as the Art Centre Project Group – without it we would not have been able to prepare our proposal or construct a manifesto to successfully work towards expanding our ideas, nor would Chapter Workshops and Centre for the Arts have got off the ground or sustained its ability to develop.

Postmodernism, together with the counterculture, was central to a cultural and social revolution that had begun in the 1960s and was evolving as we moved into the 1970s, with the arts reflecting new freedoms to express social grievances and personal liberation, for women in particular. Protest movements fought for civil rights, the women's movement, gay liberation, students for democracy, anti-war and nuclear disarmament. With the beginnings of a large-scale dismantling of the industrial base and infrastructure in areas of Wales, as well as in many other parts of Britain, communities were being abandoned to a future without any forward planning to reconstruct local economies. The reaction to these issues became subject matter for theatre productions, performance art, visual art, literature, poetry, film and video. We envisaged an arts centre that would not only reflect these social and cultural changes, but that would also be instrumental in providing spaces to support the production and presentation of innovative and new creative developments.

Between 1968 and 1970, as the Art Centre Project Group, we set up a pilot programme of events to generate interest in an art centre. Firstly, we needed to decide what kind of centre we would work towards. There had been a wide range of art labs and art centres set up throughout Britain and we decided to visit as many as possible. We travelled to the Arts Lab in Drury Lane, London which had been founded by an American, Jim Haynes, in 1967. We looked at Great Georges in Liverpool, the Birmingham Arts Lab and centres in York and Bath and the Arnolfini in Bristol which was in a converted house until it moved to Narrow Quay in Bristol harbour, and is the only one that is still functioning. However, none of the centres we visited were what we had in mind for the art centre we were planning. We then went to London to see S.P.A.C.E. (studios) set up by artists Bridget Riley and Peter Sedgley as well as musician Peter Townsend in 1968. S.P.A.C.E. based in the 'I' warehouse in St Katharine Docks, was where studio space was rented by the square foot to individual artists at affordable rents. The spaces were light and the building felt full of energy and optimism; we were particularly impressed that this was an artist-led scheme. As artists and writers ourselves we were aware that the project we were about to embark on would follow a different path to most of the other centres being proposed, because either they were led by local authorities or educational establishments. We decided at this point, whichever building we chose would need to be big enough to incorporate studios, so that we could offer artists from all disciplines the opportunity to produce and present creative work under one roof.

During this period, we approached the graphic designer Steve Allison about publicising our idea of setting up an art centre and for help with raising money. He had contacts within the music industry and the result was a twelve-hour pop festival in Sophia Gardens in Cardiff in February 1970. Pink Floyd topped the bill, supported by Black Sabbath, Quintessence and the musician and performance poet Ron Geeson. During the afternoon there were free events, which included a range of artists, craftspeople and musicians – among them were the Caricature Puppet Theatre company, the folk group Trader Horn and the mime artist Tony Crerar. I have some vivid memories of the day. The first is of travelling on the top of a double-decker bus to Sophia Gardens, looking over the walls of Bute Park and seeing a very long line of people with sleeping bags and rucksacks queueing outside Sophia Gardens Pavilion and wondering where they were going. Reality struck: I was supposed to be there taking tickets and organising the event. Other memories are of Pink Floyd refusing to perform until they were paid £600, and of counting

BROADSHEET (Cardiff University student newspaper) 17 FEBRUARY 1970

POP

ARTS CENTRE EXTRAVAGANZA

Pink Floyd

One of the biggest concerts Cardiff has known for some time took place in Sophia Gardens recently in aid of the Arts Centre Project.

The afternoon free concert included poetry readings and folk songs and Tony Crerar, a brilliant mime artist, who held the audience's attention in his invisible adventures. Trader Horne provided a powerful accompaniment to their folk songs, with auto-harp, guitar and flute. The Independent Jazz Orchestra produced an interesting abstraction of sound, whilst listening to Vaguely, an electronic sound group, was like sitting in the jungle one night when the natives are restless.

The evening performance was begun by Heaven. Here was a very much together group, whose performance was enhanced by an excellent light show, which in fact accompanied each group. Gerry Farr, although singing a fine version of 'All Along The Watchtower', lacked personality on stage and had to ask the audience to stop talking. Ron Geeson gave the impression of a mad Scottish scientist, experimenting on piano and banjo. His weird 'Stories' amused the audience and was a comic success.

Daddy Long Legs received an enthusiastic welcome from an audience obviously familiar with their material. There was full audience participation on numbers like 'I'm Getting High Again' and the group were called back for an encore. Quintessence, strongly easter influenced, sang chant-like, hypnotic songs, and were a group very much involved in their music.

Pink Floyd, the obvious top group of the evening, pleased the fans by playing much of their best material. Numbers like 'Astronomy Domine' and 'Interstellar Overdrive', show them at their gallactic best. 'Cosmos' is almost classic in magnitude and 'Careful With That Axe, Eugene' included an extra instrument, Roger Walter's throat. The group was really appreciated, and if time had permitted they would have done the encore that was called for.

The concert ended with 'Tea and Symphony' who were at a great disadvantage, coming on at 1.30 p.m. after the Floyd, but made the best of it, even with the house lights on.

COLIN REES

CARDIFF ARTS CENTRE PROJECT
BENEFIT EVENT
Thursday 5th february 5.30 — 2 a.m.
Sophia Gardens Pavilion. Cardiff

PINK FLOYD
Quintessence . Daddy Long Legs
Gary Farr . Tea & Symphony
Heaven . Black Sabbath &
Ron Geesin . Tickets 25 shillings
Free afternoon for ticketholders – 2.30 p.m.
with..TRADER HORNE . TONY CRERAR . POETRY
JAZZ . PUPPET THEATRE . MORE EVENTS

tickets from — the box office. tel. 27657
and the university union, dumfries place,
from steve allison.

Cardiff Arts Centre Project Group benefit event Festival Poster / Steve Allison ©

CARDIFF ARTS CENTRE PROJECT BENEFIT EVENT

THURSDAY, 5th FEBRUARY — 5.30-2 a.m.

SOPHIA GARDENS PAVILION, CARDIFF

PINK FLOYD

QUINTESSENCE • DADDY LONG LEGS
GARY FARR • TEA AND SYMPHONY
HEAVEN • BLACK SABBATH AND
RON GEESIN Tickets 25/-

Free afternoon Concert for ticket-holders 2.30
TRADER HORNE — TONY CRERAR — POETRY
JAZZ — PUPPET THEATRE — EVENTS

Tickets from SOPHIA GARDENS BOX OFFICE, Tel. 27657 or STEVE ALLISON, STUDENTS UNION, DUMFRIES PLACE, CARDIFF.

Cymric Federation Press, Neville Street, Cardiff.

SOUTH WALES ECHO 7 FEBRUARY 1970

POP

Festivities help arts centre plan

On The Scene, with NEIL HUGHES

Marsha Hunt — coming to Sophia Gardens next week.

THE projected arts centre for Cardiff may soon be off the ground. The 12-hour benefit concert at Sophia Gardens Pavilion on Thursday was a total success with over 1,200 people there.

For a day, it seemed as if there had been a takeover of the pavilion. Brightly dressed hippies arrived in coaches from all over South Wales and sat quietly through a long succession of first-class groups and artists.

There can be no doubt that the show was a significant success. All the artists turned up (somewhat remarkable in itself), started their spots more or less on time and played very well.

The festivities got under way early in the afternoon with poetry, movement and folk music.

Among the other events of the afternoon (which was free to ticket holders) were Trader Horne, The Independent Jazz Orchestra, mainly made up of University College, Cardiff, students, and Vaguely, a Swansea electronic sound group. There was also Black Sabbath (a Midland group), and Heaven with Gary Farr, who made a big impression at last year's Isle of Wight Festival.

We heard, too, from Ron Geesin, an eccentric somewhat obscure poet.

As well as the events on stage there were numerous side stalls and exhibitions, including a display of puppets by the Cardiff Caricature Co.

Ability

The major event of the afternoon show was certainly Tony Crerar, a mime artist who has appeared at the Round House, London.

The attraction of his act was his ability to communicate ideas of shape, size and texture to the audience simply by mime. He draws you with him into a private world. He enters the room, which is very small, finds a door, goes through and finds himself in a still smaller room and so on. A very interesting performance.

The big name artists began to take the stage at about 10 p.m. First on was Daddy Long Legs, an American band which has attracted a fair amount of attention.

During the show came one of those "happenings" that the Sunday papers are always talking about.

Slowly a translucent shape began to grow at one corner of the stage. It continued to expand until it was revealed as an inflatable polythene octopus nearly 20 feet high. Then the tentacles began to stretch out among the audience, only to collapse with a puff of compressed air, covering everyone with ribbons of plastic bag.

Quintessent, one of the most melodic of the progressive groups, were on next. One of my personal favourites. I found the interweaving of the excellent light show and their music a very relaxing and enjoyable combination.

Pink Floyd got under way in fair style with the powerful *Domino Domino*, ending their act well over an hour later with their electronic space number *Heart Of The Sun*, and their extended preview of a yet unnamed new number.

From a finance point of view it was a success. The organisers needed £1,500 to cover their costs and at 25s. a head they certainly managed that.

The profits—£500 was the figure hopefully mentioned on the night—will help to provide Cardiff with a long overdue art centre.

Theatre in Transit: with kind permission of Mike Pearson

the takings, hoping against hope that we had sold enough tickets. Over one thousand two hundred people came and the atmosphere in the Pavilion was ecstatic. Standing on the raked floor at the back of the venue and looking down at the mass of people below, with a cloud of blue smoke rising up over them, I could see many people were smoking marijuana. It was a banned drug and people could be prosecuted for allowing it to be smoked on their premises. When I turned to look at who was standing next to me I was horrified to realise it was the dreaded head of the Cardiff Drugs Squad, whose nickname was Bull Neck. He looked at me from the corner of his eye and said, 'If you keep all of this in here, I'll ignore it, but if it goes outside, I'll close you down'. It was a great relief that we did just manage to keep everything inside the Pavilion, as the alternative was unthinkable. The concert was highly successful and created a great deal of publicity, attracting a large number of people from all over Wales. We didn't make a profit; after paying for the buses to bring people down from the Valleys we barely covered our costs.

In the wake of the concert, we decided to rent an empty shop with large windows on Queen Street in the centre of Cardiff to publicise our plans and to employ a questionnaire to find out what people would like included, if an art centre were to be developed in Cardiff. During the two weeks we broadcast poetry and jazz out over Queen Street and held performances and exhibitions, including paintings by Buddhist artists from the Valleys and inflatable sculptures by Frank Triggs, a student at Cardiff Art College. Mike Pearson, performer, writer, director and academic, remembers performing with the Cardiff university student theatre group Theatre in Transit, in a wordless/mimed version of the *Odyssey* in the shop window which almost spilled out onto the street. Mike says, 'There was no specifically gathered audience – we just began and passers-by stopped to look through

pavilions in the parks
BELLE VUE PARK, NEWPORT
Six week scheme 24th JUNE — 5th AUGUST, 1970
CARDIFF CASTLE PARK, CARDIFF
Six week scheme 12th AUGUST — 16th SEPTEMBER, 1970
AN INVITATION — If you work in Drama, Environment, Event, Film, Music, Painting, Sculpture, Poetry, Sounds, Sights or Gestures, you are invited to apply for the loan of a Pavilion for one week this summer.
There will be six different types of activity at all times on six areas on the one site, with a choice of two types of Pavilion.
REQUESTS (by 1st MAY, 1970) for further details and method of application to:
PAVILIONS IN THE PARKS, Cardiff Arts Centre Project Group, 84 Kimberley Road, Cardiff, CF2 5DN.
* Work will be chosen by random draw on 12th May, 1970.

Advertisement Pavilions in the Parks

the windows and the open door, shouting comments like "Hello sailor" as we formed a boat-shaped, rocking image with Odysseus at the prow'. At the end of the two weeks, using the questionnaire as a starting point, we held a symposium at the Reardon Smith lecture theatre to discuss the findings and incorporate them into the proposal we were writing to present to Cardiff City Council. Later in the year, when we rented the Globe Cinema to show the Bob Dylan film *Don't Look Back* and *The Harder They Come*, featuring Jimmy Cliff, so many people turned up for the first screening it was impossible to find seats for everyone and we arranged other showings for those who were unable to get in the first time.

In 1970 we were asked by Peter Jones to organise and administer a scheme called Pavilions in the Parks in Belle Vue Park in Newport, Monmouthshire, and Cardiff Castle/Bute Park in Cardiff, under the auspices of the Welsh Arts Council. The first Pavilions in the Parks had been organised on Blackheath in London. The scheme entailed setting up six half-cylindrical pavilions in a cross formation in public parks, three covered in clear and three in opaque plastic. Artists were invited to apply for the pavilion that best suited their needs and the scheme attracted applications from a large number of artists from all disciplines. Pavilions in the Parks was scheduled to take place in Newport from 24th June to 5th August and in Cardiff from 12th August to 16th September 1970. During the months beforehand, we needed to follow a set process to choose which artists would

WESTERN MAIL, WEDNESDAY, MAY 20, 1970 9

Luck of the draw . . . the names of 54 artists from all over Britain are drawn from a tombola machine in Cardiff yesterday and listed by officials of an arts centre project group. There were 86 applicants for places to show their work free in special pavilions in Cardiff and Newport next month. Thirty-two of the lucky 54 artists are from Wales. They will now exhibit their work in one of six plastic pavilions which will be put up in Belle Vue Park, Newport, and Cardiff Castle Park for six weeks each from June 24. The pavilions scheme is run by Cardiff Arts Centre Project Group.

Pavilions in the Park draw

Pavilions in the Parks

take part. A separate list of artists for the clear and opaque pavilions was drawn up, the names were put into a tombola machine and pulled out by different people at random until the pavilions were filled, with another list kept in reserve in case we needed substitutes. Every space had been allocated and we were ready to open in Newport when it started to rain, and it rained and rained until the whole site was a quagmire. To make matters worse, the park warden would switch off the electricity when he decided we were getting too noisy or if he didn't approve of the artist; this was extremely disappointing for all the people involved. As a result, it was with great trepidation we approached the opening of Pavilions in the Parks in Cardiff, but the situation could not have been a greater contrast. From the first day the sun shone, and for the whole of the time visual and performance artists worked for one week in each pavilion and members of the public came to see the work free of charge; all in all, it was a very successful and memorable event. This scheme was the first of its kind in Wales and gave us enough confidence to move on to the next phase of our plans.

Bradnum Building, Custom House St, Cardiff

The question of a building to house the art centre had been in the forefront of our minds during 1969. We had looked at a range of disused industrial buildings throughout Cardiff and decided to choose the Bradnum building on Custom House Street in the city centre as the strongest possibility. In our proposal, written during that year, we laid out in detail how we planned to convert, finance, administer and utilise the building. Indeed, we weren't far

ARTS CENTRE

SUCCESS AT LAST!

There must be many people in Cardiff who, although enthusiastic about the idea of an arts centre, never really believed it would become a reality. I must admit that at times I began to have my doubts, when the negotiations with the council and the search for premises seemed to go on and on.

But now the opening of the centre is getting nearer and nearer—in the autumn you will be able to actually go to a building (which for the sake of convenience we'll call the Arts Centre here—we intend to give it a name of its own by the time we open) and there paint, rehearse, listen to music, watch films, hear poetry or just talk with other people, following your own interest and perhaps finding new ones.

The old Canton High School in Market Road, Canton, is the building we shall transform into the Arts Centre. There are some 29,000 square feet available and plans are being drawn up to utilise this place to its best advantage. As it is an existing building, there are certain limits to what can be done; but as it was a school we are not having to contend with vast open areas and a great deal of modification. The basic services, power and plumbing, are already there and in sound order—although one does wonder what to do with dozens of child-size toilets! The conversion will be based on the answers given in the questionnaire sent to potential users of the Centre—from these answers we can assess the type of space required, the nature of the performance areas, the facilities needed, any special requirements and so on.

The Arts Centre Project Group has joined with the Cardiff Civic Theatre Group to negotiate with the council and to work out the details of conversion and organisation of the Centre. The steering committee of eight formed through this co-operation has now reached the point where it is dealing with details rather than general plans, the legal problems of the formation of a Charitable Trust, the drawing up of the lease and so on.

Things are now moving quickly—when you come back next session you will find the Centre (whatever we finally decide to call it) there—and we hope that its existence will only be the beginning of a new growth of the artistic activity in Cardiff.

LIZ WESTON

Old Canton High School, headquarters for the Arts Centre

Page 8 BROADSHEET

COUNCIL TO SUPPORT ARTS CENTRE

Liz Weston

In a report submitted to Cardiff Corporation, the Arts Centre Project Group stressed the need for immediate action to be taken in housing the arts in Cardiff and South Wales. Unless this is done, even as a short-term measure, the planners will be unable to assess the size and design of the building that would be required when they eventually build their proposed centre in the 1980's.

ARGUMENT

The argument that a short-term centre would act as a working blueprint for the future and that it was essential to encourage and nurture the arts now, impressed the planners and the Corporation are now making definite proposals outlining the role they would play in the establishment of the stop-gap centre. This is the first time during the months of talks that we have had concrete statements from the officials—a very encouraging sign. A short-list of buildings suitable for conversion has been drawn up and representatives of the Arts Centre Project Group and the Civic Theatre Trust will be looking at the schools and other buildings the Corporation have suggested.

BUILDING

The advantages of taking over a building, such as a school, owned by Cardiff Corporation are obvious—we would be negotiating directly with a sympathetic party; a school would already have power and plumbing installed and it would be in a satisfactory state of repair—thus cutting out a large capital outlay by the Group.

If any one of these buildings proves satisfactory we would immediately open negotiations for occupation, from then on it will be entirely up to us how quickly the Centre was opened. We are determined to act as swiftly as possible — our argument to the officials has always been "Give us a building today and you'll have an Arts Centre tomorrow."

NEXT PLAN

What is the Group planning to do next? After the success of the Sophia Gardens event (for want of a better word for the twelve hours of music, poetry, mime and things that went on there) we will probably arrange another similar venture in the future; but our immediate plans are for a week-long arts centre to be set up in a disused building in the city, with exhibitions, lunch - time concerts and rush-hour events. And quite soon a theatre event involving some of the best theatre groups in the country.

Exciting things are planned for the summer too—so keep a look out for further news.

Cardiff is beginning to wake up and we hope to prevent it from nodding-off again.

Newspaper articles

off the mark in the way things turned out, but not in the Bradnum building. Initially, we had proposed our art centre would be a working blue-print for the Centreplan 70 Art and Cultural Centre to be built in Cardiff city centre by Ravenseft Properties Ltd, who had previously redeveloped Birmingham city centre in the 1960s. This changed when the scheme that had been commissioned by the Conservative city council to redevelop Cardiff was overturned by a Labour council, led by Paddy Kitson, in 1973. It was realised that the proposed scheme would destroy much of the Victorian architecture, including the Arcades, and a multiple-lane highway around the castle would change the landscape of the city. I was invited to be an artistic adviser to the Labour working party considering this scheme and was in total agreement that these plans should be abandoned, even though there was a very large compensation fee paid to Ravenseft. Looking at the proposed plan now, it shows how the Victorian buildings that grace the main street of Cardiff's unique city centre would have been changed into steel and glass structures with overhead walkways. This, in my opinion, would have been disastrous, as we would have lost one of the most beautiful capital cities in Europe.

Encouraged by the success of our pilot schemes, we summoned up our courage to ask for a meeting with City Council members to discuss the possibility of renting a disused, corporation-owned building. Three disused buildings were suggested: a junior school on Crwys Road, the fire station in Dumfries Place, and Canton High School. If the building was going to accommodate everything, we planned to offer in the art centre,

Canton High School was the place. The building had been condemned and uninhabited for a few years, as the council had plans to demolish it. Although the services were in a poor state of repair, with much of the electric wiring, as well as many windows and lead flashing from the roof, missing, as soon as we saw inside we knew the 42,958 square feet of space on two floors was where everything we planned to offer in the art centre could begin to take shape. The other major factor in making our decision was that the building was in Canton, a busy working-class area of Cardiff. We arranged a meeting with the Leader of the City Council in his office in City Hall to tell him we had decided on Canton High School. He sat behind his mahogany desk as we stood before him and told him of our plans – he was somewhat less than enthusiastic and thumped the desk saying, 'We don't support lame ducks and I give you six months'. The fact he was agreeing to lease this council-owned building to two artists and a writer in their twenties, with no experience in management or major building projects, said a great deal about him, the City Council and the age we were living in. Having signed a lease which included a 'peppercorn' rent on Canton High School, initially for a year, we needed to decide what to do with all this derelict space and how to convert it into an art centre with absolutely no money. Somehow, we didn't see it as a problem: we were just going to give it our all to make it work and that was that.

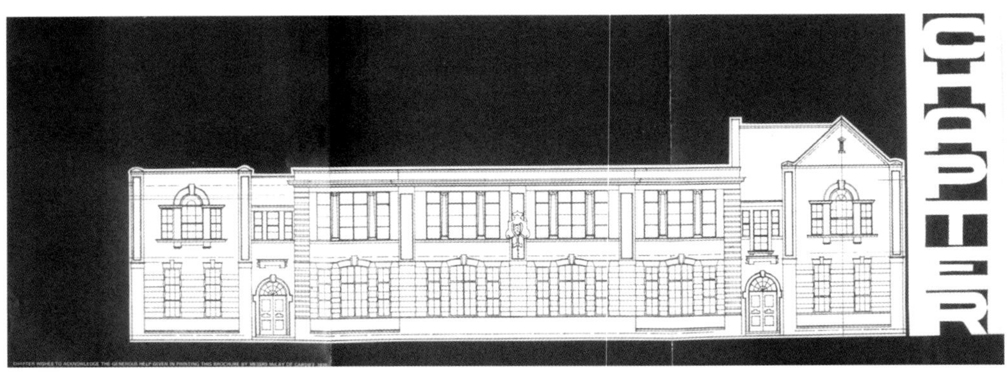

Chapter Arts Centre Brochure
– Designer Bryan Jones

Arts centres, especially artist-led centres, were a new phenomenon at the time and we, as the Arts Centre Project Group, were very conscious we should not impose one view of how the arts should develop; instead, we should respond to the needs which were being expressed by the artists. From the outset, we planned to establish an environment in which all creative disciplines could be housed, and to encourage, nurture and support the making of all art forms under one roof, through the provision of studio, rehearsal and editing spaces. Our objective was to generate ideas between the arts; this formed the basis from which the studios, galleries, theatres and cinemas grew. The way these spaces

Chapter's first membership card – Designer Bryan Jones

developed was in response to the need of each creative activity in the building; we recognised this was a unique opportunity to expand connections, overcome any perceived barriers between disciplines and open channels of communication between different art forms, so that links could be forged. Underpinning this was our belief that all aspects of the creative spirit would flourish in an atmosphere of understanding and co-operation. Chapter was the first arts centre in Wales as well as the foremost arts organisation to support the concept of Postmodernism.

Just after we moved into Canton High School in December 1970, Alan Saunders, a member of the Everyman amateur theatre group, volunteered as our solicitor. Alan advised us to become a limited company with charitable trust status, and at an evening meeting in his office, Bryan, Mik and I were told that for the arts centre to be set up with this structure we would need to appoint a board and that all the members of the arts centre would become shareholders in the company. To complete the forms we were asked us to choose a name. We hadn't ever thought about this question, but Bryan suggested 'Chapter' and, given the urgency of making a decision, Mik and I agreed; it's a decision I've never regretted. Alan worked tirelessly with us and his support was a major factor in the survival of Chapter in the early years.

Between the time we moved into Canton High School in late 1970 and Chapter being registered as a company and a charitable trust on 23th March 1971, many changes and developments had taken place. Julie (Jules) had joined us when she and Mik moved into the schoolhouse next to Chapter. We had begun to convert areas into studios and were planning a gallery, performance space, cinemas and a bar; throughout this time we were in contact with professional artists and the centre began to evolve. As the building work continued in Chapter, our concerns were two-fold: to encourage professional artists from all disciplines to move into the spaces to produce and present their art, and also to ensure the local community was encouraged to use the building as much as possible. The first area of the building was designated for studios and we advertised them to be rented by the

Julie and Nothing the dog extraordinaire

Cinema 2 Photo Cine Society

square foot. We were amazed at the response: in a short space of time painters, printmakers, sculptors, ceramicists, musical instrument makers and artists working in multidisciplinary ways had moved in. One of the first artists to take up residency was the extraordinary sculptor and painter Charles Byrd, who continued painting and making 'Magical Machine' constructions, as well as paying regular visits to Chapter, until he was one hundred and one years of age. The first artists and craft workers included: violin maker Don Tatum, painter/painting restorer John Dawson Evans, weaver Ann Gladstone, illustrator Jenny Hewison, musician Suzi Greengrass, potter Brian Giles, printmaker Anthony Davies and painter Alan Wood.

We were very aware that we needed to earn an income from the building to support developing a professional arts programme; therefore, we also rented space to amateur groups like the South Wales Arts Society, the Everyman theatre group and Cardiff Cine Society. Brian Bull and other members of the cine society led the way by converting two children's cloakrooms into one of the best small cinema spaces in south Wales, which still exists as Cinema Two. In tandem with this, we began to convert classrooms into the Gallery and our own cinema, which was furnished with equipment from a cinema in the Valleys; we believed that the cinema would be a key feature in bringing people into the building. Another way to achieve our aim of creating a link between the development of the arts taking place and our local community was to rent space to the Workers Educational Association (WEA), which ran regular courses. Tutors in the WEA gave us vital support throughout the early years, among them politician Rhodri Morgan and city councillor Paddy Kitson. I considered it very important that local schools were involved and began to run workshops in conjunction with exhibitions in the Gallery. This was a new concept at the time and there was a wonderful response from both Radnor and Severn Road Primary Schools in Canton. We invited local mothers to run a nursery school, believing that if young children were involved with activities in the building, they would grow up accepting the arts as a natural part of everyday life. Over the past 50 years it has been a great privilege to meet people who came to the nursery school and who now bring their children and grandchildren to Chapter.

Poster Designed by Christine Kinsey

We also rented meeting rooms in Chapter to other groups, including a summer school for Gypsy children, Hare Krishna gatherings, Cardiff Yacht Club, a Shelter conference and the Campaign for Homosexual Equality (CHE). During this time Chapter's

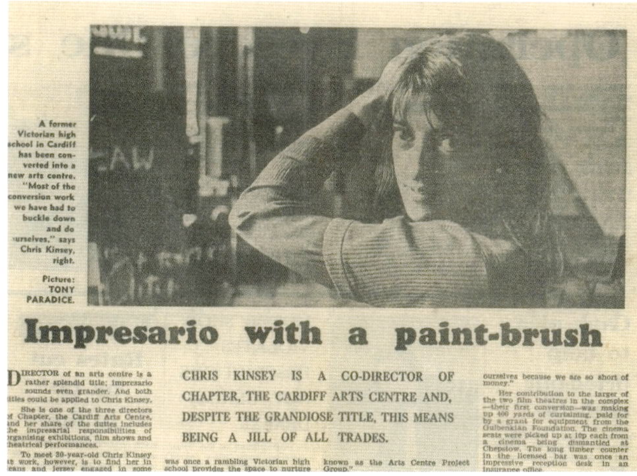

A former Victorian high school in Cardiff has been converted into a new arts centre. "Most of the conversion work we have had to buckle down and do ourselves," says Chris Kinsey, right.

Picture: TONY PARADICE.

Impresario with a paint-brush

DIRECTOR of an arts centre is a rather splendid title; impresario sounds even grander. And both titles could be applied to Chris Kinsey.

She is one of the three directors of Chapter, the Cardiff Arts Centre, and her share of the duties includes the impresarial responsibilities of organising exhibitions, film shows and theatrical performances.

To meet 30-year-old Chris Kinsey at work, however, is to find her in jeans and jersey engaged in some

CHRIS KINSEY IS A CO-DIRECTOR OF CHAPTER, THE CARDIFF ARTS CENTRE AND, DESPITE THE GRANDIOSE TITLE, THIS MEANS BEING A JILL OF ALL TRADES.

was once a rambling Victorian high school provides the space to nurture

known as the Arts Centre Project Group."

ourselves because we are so short of money."

Her contribution to the larger of the two film theatres in the complex —their first conversion—was making up 400 yards of curtaining, paid for by a grant for equipment from the Gulbenkian Foundation. The cinema seats were picked up at 10p each from a cinema being dismantled at Chepstow. The long timber counter in the licensed bar was once an impressive reception desk in an insurance office.

Western Mail article
– Photograph Christine Kinsey

work in such areas was controversial and sometimes attracted hostile coverage from the press and adverse reactions from some councillors. One of the headlines in a Welsh daily paper in 1971 announced 'Old Canton High School taken over by Long Haired Communists and Homosexuals' while another article published in the *Daily Telegraph* was entitled 'Homosexual club Aided by Council', referring to Cardiff City Council. When Chapter was threatened with closure for holding a Shelter conference and CHE meetings, Mike Jarrett, who was the convenor of Cardiff CHE and later became Chair of Chapter Board, was working with us, and although we needed to curtail some of our activities for a short while to keep Chapter open, we soon went back to welcoming these organisations. I am extremely proud that over the years Chapter has led the way to support minority and marginalised groups and has pursued gender and sexual equality in all its activities and programming. I knew if Chapter did not reflect the diversity of society and community life, together with building connections between artists and the wider public, it would fail, as sadly, was the fate of many other centres in subsequent years. Of course, these were very important issues for us, but our main purpose was to support professional artists by creating the spaces for new and experimental work.

Old Canton High School
work in progress

It was often daunting to imagine how we were going to raise money, not only to convert 42,958 square feet of derelict space but also to fund a programme of events. We were awarded a grant of £2,500 from the Welsh Arts Council and initially the City Council charged us a peppercorn rent of £1,000 per year. Bryan and I had given up our teaching jobs and Mik was no longer working as a freelance writer, which meant we suffered severe personal financial problems. But the enthusiasm and energy of people around us and the exciting possibilities we could see ahead carried us through. From the beginning it was our intention that, once Chapter was up and running, we would return to our own work, but of course this did not happen: there were far too many things to do. Nevertheless, I think we all felt those early years were extremely creative. As new artists joined us and the building developed

Chapter Gallery (three converted classrooms)

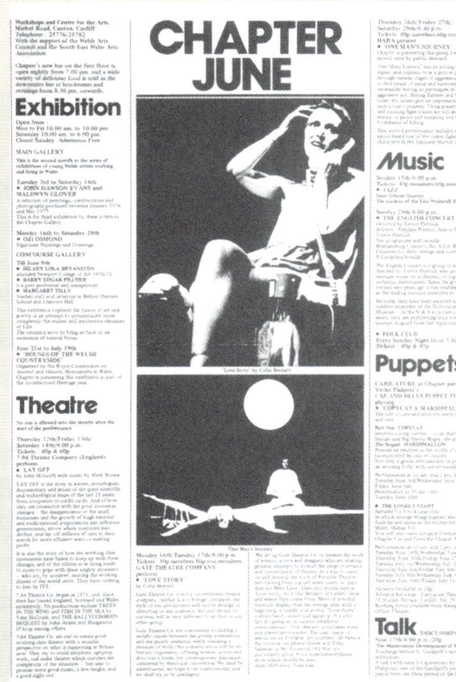

Chapter Event Sheets Chapter May Event sheet designed by Peter Gill, Design Systems.
All other designs by Bryan Jones and Christine Kinsey

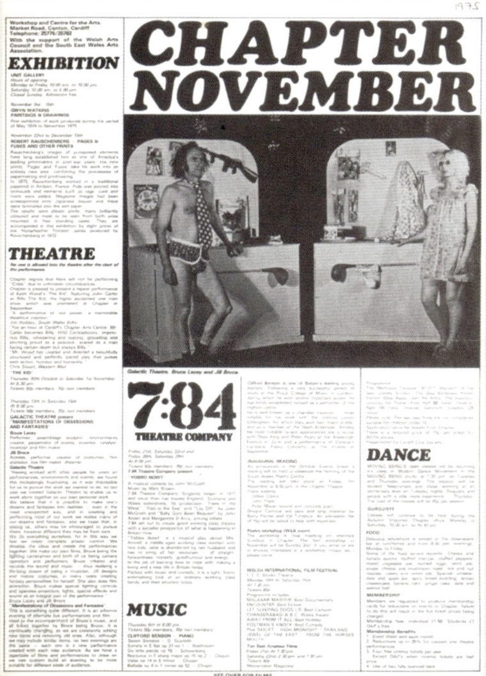

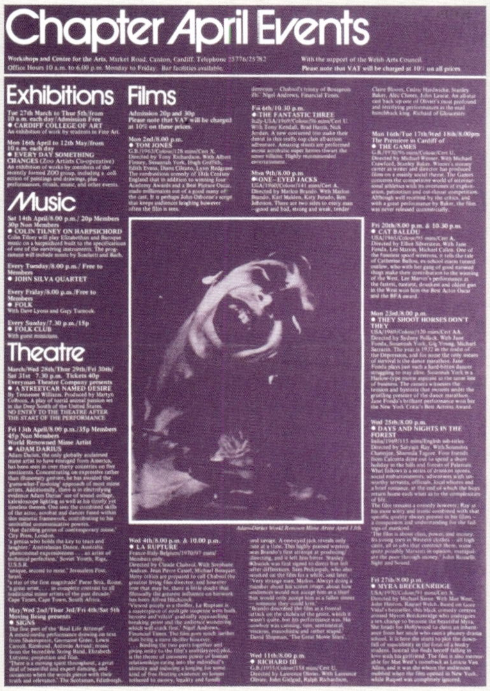
Chapter April Events
Exhibitions
Films
Music
Theatre

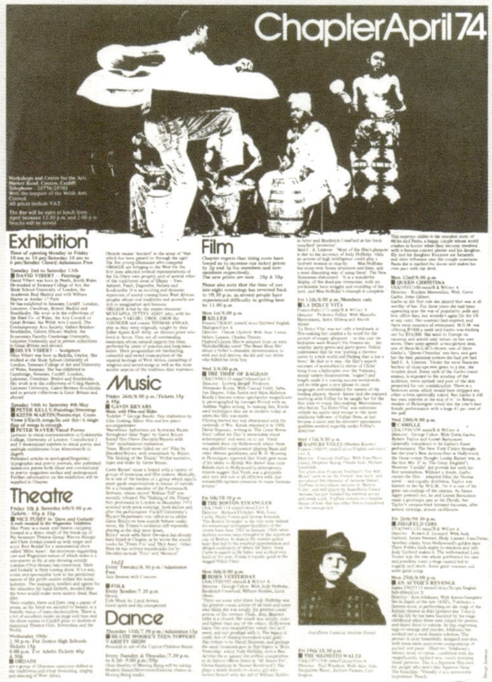
ChapterApril74
Exhibition
Film
Music
Theatre
Dance

CHAPTER APRIL
Exhibition
Theatre
Music
Dance

CHAPTER DECEMBER
Exhibition
Theatre
Films
Music
Dance

CHAPTER MARCH
EXHIBITION
MUSIC
THEATRE
FILM
POETRY

January Chapter
Film
Theatre
Poetry
Music
Exhibition

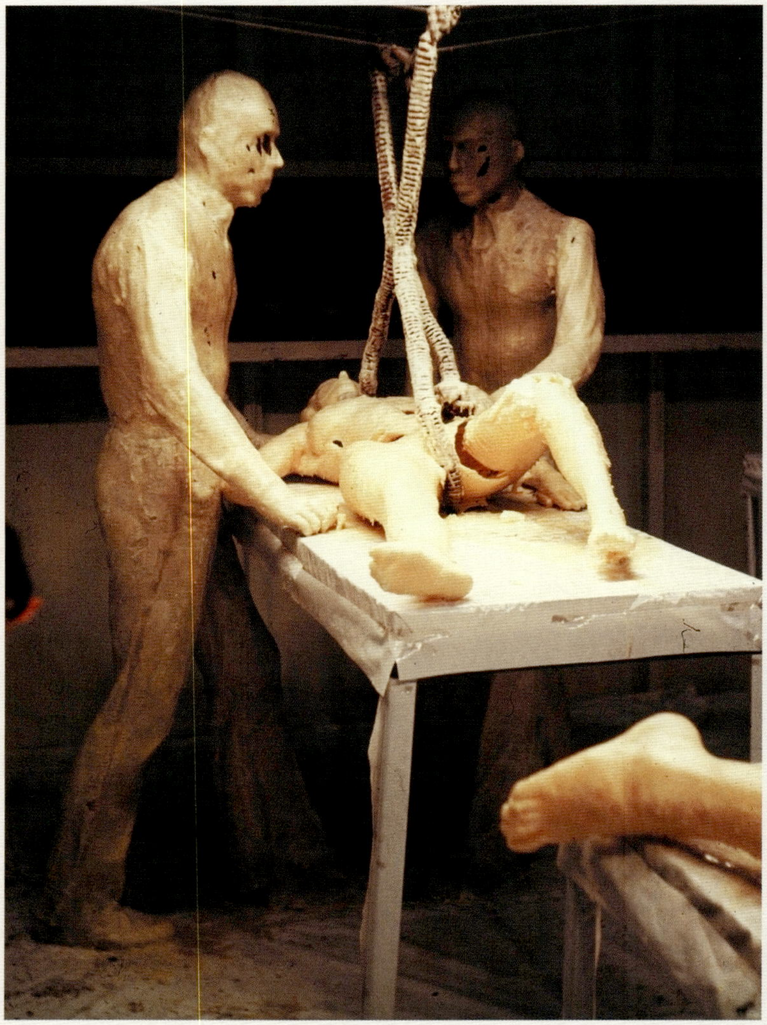

Poster design by Peter Gill, Design Systems /
Photographs of Peter Dockley Installation

of local residents was a slow process, but we were determined that Chapter would be identified with Canton rather than seen as an 'ivory tower' of artists. Misrepresentation and unfavourable local press coverage, together with a few local councillors who were determined to close Chapter down, often made this very difficult.

As the programme of events began to develop, we needed to advertise and approached Peter Gill at Design Systems; he generously agreed to sponsor Chapter, not only designing the initial event sheet but continued to design each monthly printed programme throughout the first year, setting the high standard for design and print we had hoped for. I knew it was essential to present Chapter to the wider world as an organisation that aimed to promote professional creative artists through high quality publicity. Bryan and I took over from Peter and continued designing event sheets, posters and flyers for events, as well as brochures, invitations and membership cards, all of which we did in between our other work. Some of our graphics documenting the cultural and social history of Chapter, as it developed during the early years, are now in the Chapter archive at the National Library of Wales, Aberystwyth, with others in the Victoria and Albert Museum, London.

During this time, influenced by Postmodernism, artists were moving away from the Modernist ethos that mainly concentrated on painting and traditional sculpture. Our aim was to create spaces where visual art could come down from walls and off plinths to inhabit spaces that physically took the viewer into another world. Chapter's first commissioned work, in March 1972, was a remarkable installation by sculptor Peter Dockley and performance artist John Hart, which epitomised the direction many artists were following in the Postmodernist revolution. The installation and performance took place in an eight-foot-high wooden room we constructed in the centre of the downstairs hall. It had a narrow window along each wall where the audience was able to see into the room. Lying on two tables were full-size wax figures of people impregnated with seeds. One of the figures was in a cage together with rats, while the other figure had chickens eating the seeds. Peter and John entered the room, covered in wax, and at different times of the day they worked on the figures with gas fire torches. Over a period of weeks the wax figures on the tables slowly disintegrated as the seeds were being eaten and the wax melted. The work was a sensation, because for many people it was the first time they had experienced visual art as performance. Chapter's Gallery programme continued to provide alternative spaces for happenings, concrete poetry, and performance, destructive, conceptual, minimal and kinetic art, as well as painting, print, photography, sculpture and documentary exhibitions. This programme reflected the radical changes the counterculture and Postmodernism had made on the visual arts from the 1960s into the 1970s.

Joseph Herman poster designed by Peter Gill, Design Systems / Other posters designed by Bryan Jones and Christine Kinsey

Posters designed by Bryan Jones and Christine Kinsey

Posters designed by Bryan Jones
and Christine Kinsey

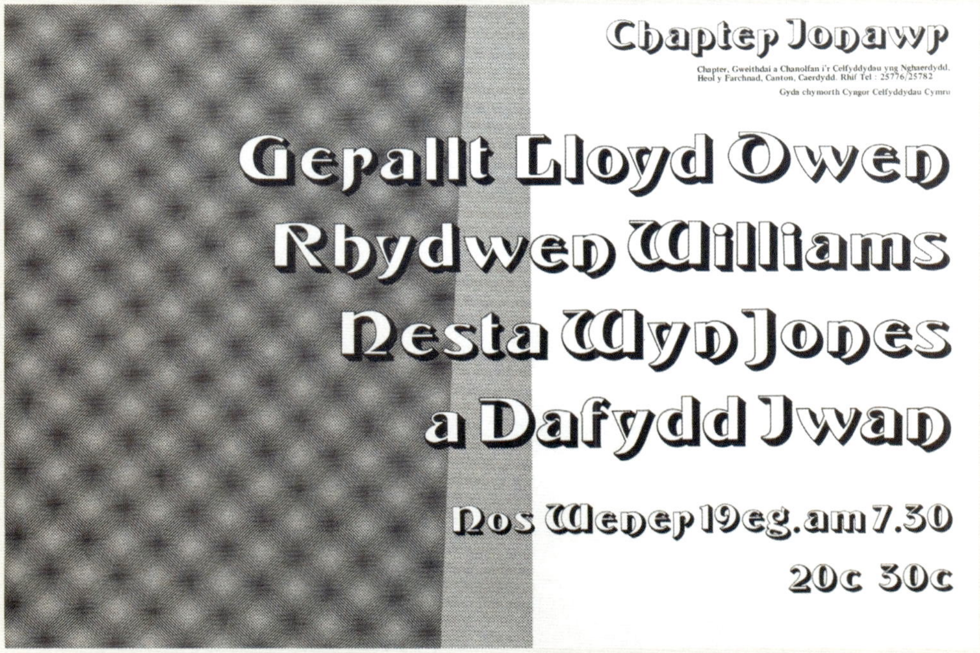

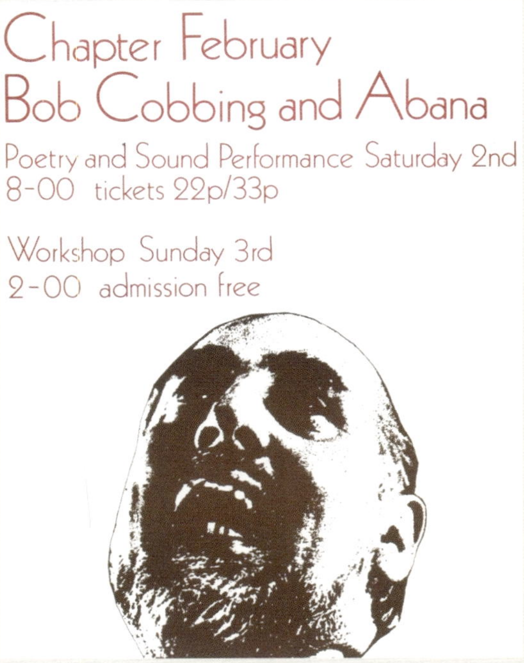

Posters designed by Bryan Jones and Christine Kinsey

The lack of recognition of women in all aspects of the creative arts was apparent during Modernism but this began to change slowly throughout the 1960s and into the 1970s when feminists demanded that their voices were heard. In May 1976 we hosted a month-long Festival of Women in the Arts in which we were able to offer opportunities to professional women artists in theatre, dance, poetry, film and the visual arts. An exhibition of women visual artists called *Five Women Artists: Images of Womanpower* included a painting by Monica Sjöö called *God Giving Birth* (1968), depicting a woman, who filled the large canvas, at the point of giving birth. Because the painting was considered blasphemous, once again Chapter was threatened with being closed down if we did not remove the work from the exhibition. A group of councillors had been designated to inspect the painting, which was hung in the end gallery and could be seen immediately as they walked in. We were fortunate that Chapter was at a stage where we had gained the support of more city councillors and after a great deal of discussion, I was able to persuade them that this painting should remain in the exhibition.

Moving Being, a multi-media theatre company founded by Geoff Moore, moved into Chapter during the Summer of 1972 from their previous base at the Contemporary School of Dance in London. Mary Mumford, the administrator, had come to Cardiff in the spring to discuss an invitation from the University of Wales to become part of their Arts programme. When we met Mary, we knew immediately that Moving Being would be the perfect theatre company to make a home in Chapter. Geoff Moore, the director of Moving Being, used interweaving art forms as the basis of his creative work and together with designer Peter Mumford and costume designer/performer Pam Moore, worked with professional actors, contemporary dancers, musicians and visual artists to produce some of the most exciting and innovative theatre in Britain at the time. A symbiotic and mutually beneficial relationship developed between the company and Chapter, as the work was at the core of our vision for the Arts Centre. Geoff later said in an interview with Heike Roms, researcher, academic and author of *What's Welsh for Performance?* that 'Chapter provided the perfect context with an abundance of usable space, other interesting and committed artists, and a sense that everything was possible'. The inspirational production *Phoenix* (1972) was followed by *Signs, Angels, Sun,* a trilogy with the overall title *The Real Life Attempt* (1973) and *Dreamplay* (1974), an August Strindberg play which had fascinated me in Newport College of Art. These were some of the first performances by a company in Wales to fuse contemporary dance, film, the spoken word and music. I often think about these performances and have come to realise how influential the imagery has been on my work. Between 1974 and 1977 Geoff Moore and Moving Being went on to make many successful productions. The company made an

Photographs and posters Moving Being with kind permission of Geoff Moore and Peter Mumford

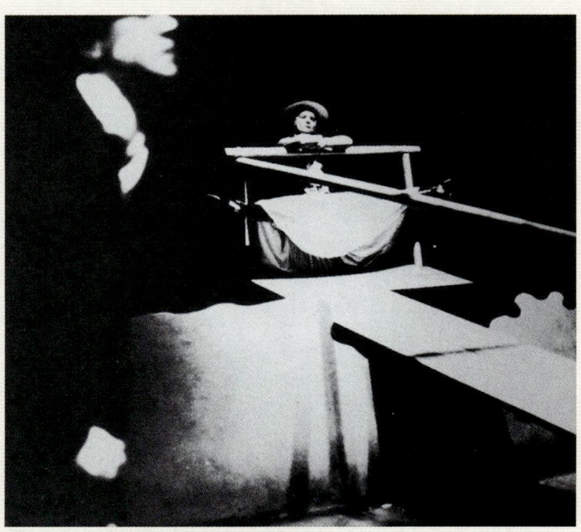

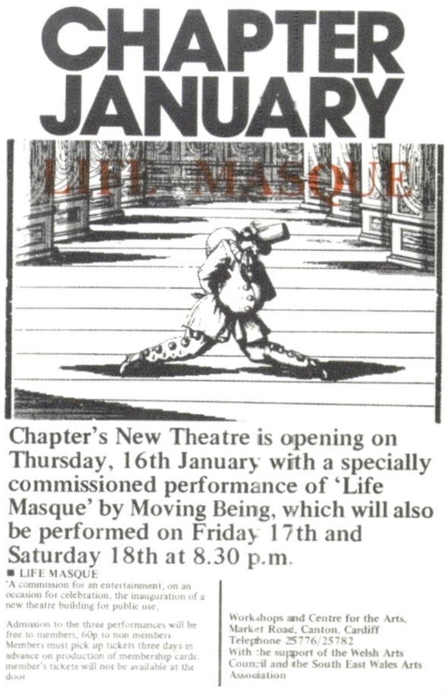

CHAPTER JANUARY

Chapter's New Theatre is opening on Thursday, 16th January with a specially commissioned performance of 'Life Masque' by Moving Being, which will also be performed on Friday 17th and Saturday 18th at 8.30 p.m.

■ LIFE MASQUE

'A commission for an entertainment, on an occasion for celebration, the inauguration of a new theatre building for public use,

Admission to the three performances will be free to members, 60p to non members. Members must pick up tickets three days in advance on production of membership cards: member's tickets will not be available at the door.

Workshops and Centre for the Arts, Market Road, Canton, Cardiff
Telephone 25776/25782
With the support of the Welsh Arts Council and the South East Wales Arts Association

immense contribution to the success of Chapter as a national and international centre for the arts.

When Moving Being arrived in Chapter there was no purpose-built theatre space. Peter Mumford initially designed a temporary theatre space on the ground floor; this included a steel structure to support raked seating, made by Lynden Lewis, and a lighting control box built under the guidance of Peter Clark, a structural engineer. By 1974 we were able to raise enough money to move the theatre to a permanent place on the first floor, which was opened on 15th January 1975 by the great Joan Littlewood and a performance of *Life Masque* by Moving Being, as a specially commissioned work. We had worked tirelessly to complete the theatre on time, but on the day it opened Joan Littlewood arrived earlier than expected and I was still on my hands and knees laying carpet tiles in the theatre foyer as she walked up the stairs. Her reaction was completely empathetic, referring to her own experience at Theatre Royal Stratford East, and she was very complimentary about the theatre and what we had achieved.

Improving the facilities of the theatre space made it possible for Chapter to promote resident companies. Cardiff Laboratory for Theatrical Research was founded by Richard Gough and Mike Pearson in 1974, it became one of the most influential theatre companies in Wales and began its connection with Chapter by performing in the theatre downstairs. Later in the 1970s the group changed their name to Cardiff Laboratory Theatre and moved into the Gym, an annex next to the main Chapter building, and continued to produce highly innovative and often provocative work. Its successor, the Centre for Performance

Photographs Cardiff Laboratory for Theatrical Research with kind permission of Mike Pearson

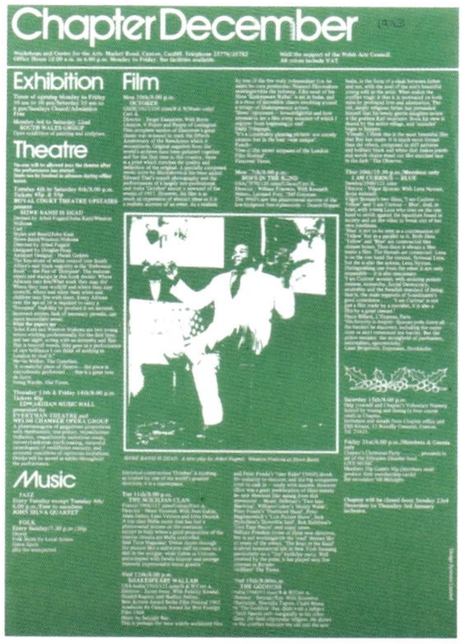

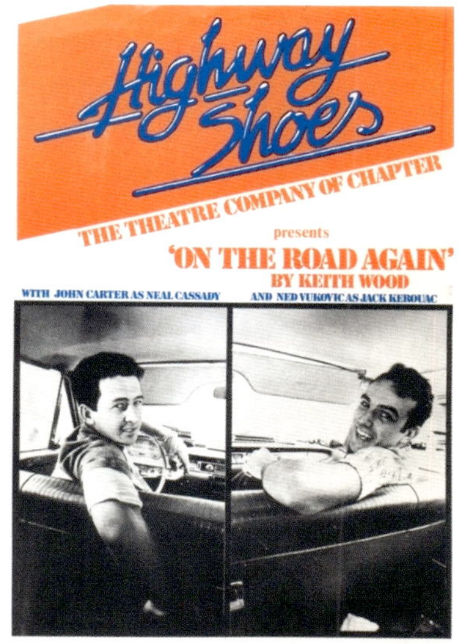

Posters left and right designed by Bryan Jones and Christine Kinsey / Poster in the centre Paupers Carnival – Dek Leverton and Vanya Constant

Research, formed in Aberystwyth 1988 continued to promote emerging artists and highly acclaimed theatre productions. Other theatre groups such as Paupers Carnival with Vanya Constant and Dek Leverton and the Keith Wood Production Company – Highway Shoes took up residence in the building between 1974 and 1976. In 1978 Janek Alexander founded his own theatre group, Diamond Age, and wrote and performed in eight productions. He became Chapter's theatre programmer and subsequently the greatly respected Director in 1996. It was always our intention that Chapter would host major events in all the arts. In 1977 the eminent residency project *Woyzeck* by the Pip Simmons Group took over the whole building, and a full-size swimming pool was constructed in Chapter's yard. We supported many other experimental national and international theatre companies, as well as the growing interest in contemporary dance. It was important for Chapter to offer audiences an opportunity to see all aspects of performance in contemporary theatre.

There were very many memorable performances, one of the most moving and poignant was *Sizwe Bansi is Dead* in December 1973, written and performed by Winston Ntshona and John Kani in collaboration with the writer Athol Fugard, who were all members of the Serpent Players from South Africa. We hosted the play at very short notice after it had been premiered in the Royal Court Theatre in London in 1972. *Sizwe Bansi is Dead* is about the discrimination created by the passbook system and its effect on lives of black South Africans. The actors were performing outside South Africa for the first time, putting themselves in great danger if they returned to their country. John Kani and Winston Ntshona were in Chapter for a week. On one of those days, while I was covering a wall with cork tiles to make a notice board, Winston helped me to complete the job. We had a conversation about South Africa which I will never forget. At this time a new wave of Welsh writing for theatre was coming to the fore. Alan Osborne, an artist, writer and composer was a fellow student at Newport College of Art. He is one of Wales' most significant playwrights whose work explores his experience of growing up in the mining and steel-making town of Merthyr Tydfil in the South Wales Valleys. One of his first productions was his seminal opera *Terraces* which used the whole of the Chapter building,

Left – Poster with kind permission of Alan Osborne / Right – Poster designed by Christine Kinsey

followed by *The Merthyr Trilogy – Bull, Nut and Rock, In Sunshine and in Shadow, Redemption Song* as well as *Slaughter on Grand Avenue*. These productions paved the way for new writers in Welsh theatre and an extraordinary series of plays supported by Gilly Adams through the Made in Wales theatre production company based in the Sherman Theatre.

A very active Poetry Society met in the bar each week with readings by Welsh and international poets. I often read Yevgeny Yevtushenko's poetry, especially his poem *Lies*, and so was delighted when he came to Chapter. The evening became even more significant than expected, when a group of women, protesting against the way Jews were being treated in Russia, blocked the stairs to the theatre just as Yevgeny arrived. He took time to speak to the group and then read his poems, which took on an even greater meaning.

The musician and musicologist Judith Serota volunteered to organise a programme of music in 1973. With her expertise, she introduced audiences to both rarely heard early music and contemporary composers. In 1975–1976 for example, 13 concerts were organised; these featured a wide range of composers and performers, some of whom had not been heard in Cardiff previously. Judith made an invaluable contribution to Chapter and the musical life of Cardiff.

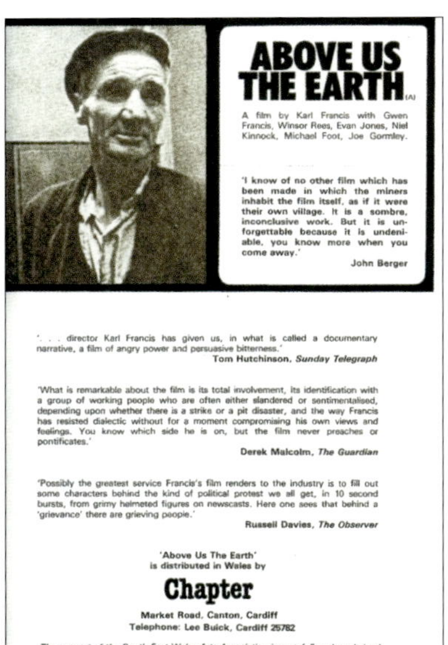

Poster with kind permission of Karl Francis

Film played a crucial role in Chapter's development, establishing an audience as well as an important cash flow. We showed a mixture of commercial successes, and avant-garde continental and New Wave films, with the former subsidising less popular work. Supporting emerging film-makers was very important to us; Christopher Monger, after directing his student film *Cold Mountain*, set up Chapter Film Workshop with cameraman Roland Denning and producer Laurie McFadden in 1973, the only one of its kind in Wales at the time. Karl Francis' salient docudrama film *Above Us the Earth* (1977) was made in association with Chapter Film Workshop and distributed in Wales by Chapter. It exposed the injustice of pit closures in the Rhymney Valley during the 1970s; filmed at Ogilvie Colliery, it featured artist, writer, teacher and cultural activist Osi Rhys Osmond. Karl Francis produced a series of films showing the exploitation of miners in the South Wales Valleys including *A Case for Coal* and *Rumours at the Miners' Fortnight*, both made by the local pitmen themselves. These films laid bare the generations of people in the South Wales Valleys whose personal lives had been dominated by the profiteering of industrial companies. Karl's remarkable film-making career is explored in his book *Encounters with Karl Francis*.[2]

One of the first workshops we set up was a darkroom, which provided a facility to serve many of the artists and organisations who rented studios in the building and also the local community. The Print Workshop empowered inexperienced individuals and social groups to create graphics in the workshops, producing high-quality material to communicate their messages. For many professional artists at this time, Agitprop, as a form of political activism, was the basis of their creativity and Chapter was able to facilitate their work, while our social programme continued to support other areas that encouraged community involvement.

Poster Charles Byrd Exhibition designed by Bryan Jones

Chapter's first birthday party in 1973 was an extravaganza of sound and colour. Charles Byrd's Magical Machines whirled and twirled exuberantly in the Gallery and Bruce Lacey and Jill Bruce performed with the Bonzo Dog Doo Dah Band. Peter Kuttner made and presented red, blue and green spaghetti bolognese and bread as well as five enormous cakes, including a birthday cake and one in the form of a coffin, all of which were offered to the audience and eaten by those who braved the visual appearance. The Bath Theatre Workshop created clouds of brightly coloured billowing smoke in and around the very large crowd who had come to celebrate Chapter's first year of full operation.

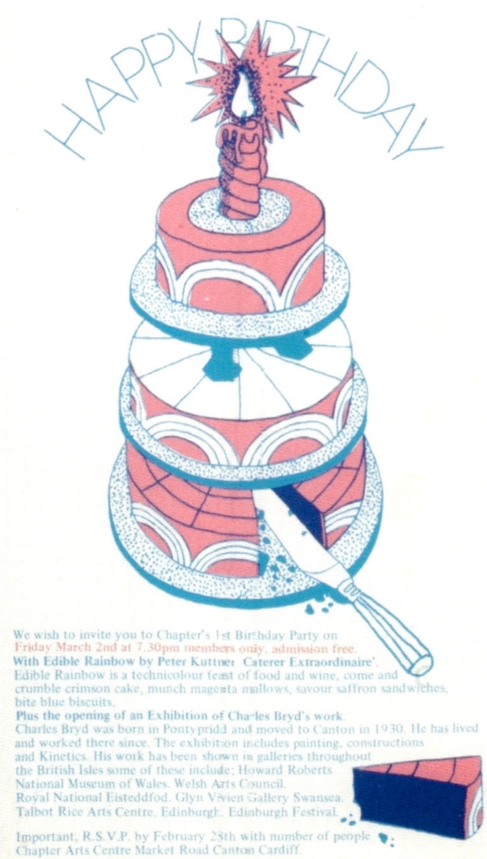

Chapter's First Birthday invitation card designed by Bryan Jones and Christine Kinsey

When the Arts Council of Great Britain commissioned their senior researcher, Robert Hutchinson, to report on arts centres, Chapter was one of those he selected. He took the year 1975/76 as the basis for his research, spending two weeks in Chapter compiling the information. The report was initially on four arts centres but ultimately published as *Three Arts Centres*, because we were told, the administrators of Great Georges, Liverpool would not agree to have a report on them included in the publication. The other two arts centres were South Hill Park, Bracknell, run by the local authority, and Gardner Centre for the Arts, affiliated to the University of Sussex. Chapter was the only artist-led centre and Hutchinson criticised aspects of Chapter that didn't fit into the research criteria, which did not include a category for assessing artist-led arts centres like Chapter that had grown organically by

Posters designed by Bryan Jones and Christine Kinsey

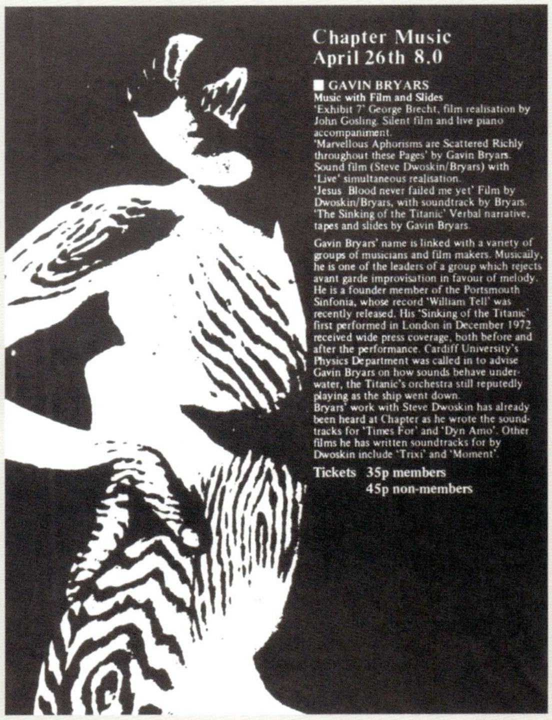

responding to the requirements of artists in the building who were developing new art forms. He did not understand how we managed to organise a full programme of events and administer the whole organisation on a very small budget with so few members of staff, and relying on the goodwill of volunteers to support our work. However, in his review of the programme for the year, Hutchinson records what makes amazing reading now. In the 1975/1976 financial year Chapter hosted 10 exhibitions in the gallery, 30 productions/performances in the theatre, showed three films a week in Cinema One, totalling 150 different feature films, in total attracting audiences of more than thirty thousand. He remarked in his report: 'Indeed Yevtushenko, Princess Margaret, Lord Radcliffe Maud, John McGrath, the Marchioness of Anglesey and Bruce Lacey have at least one thing in common – they all visited Chapter in 1975–1976'. We agreed to the publication of the report because we wanted to make our case that independent, artist-led centres needed to be judged by a more appropriate set of criteria.

Our programming of events in Chapter was intended to provide a window on Wales and a doorway into the world of contemporary cultural developments. We tried to show a good proportion of the extraordinary developing art forms that were being produced in Wales including in the Welsh language and also reflect major changes which were taking place in the wider arts world. Artists from all disciplines required different spaces and environments to present the new ideas being formulated by cultural and social alternative situations, and Chapter, with its flexible administrative structure and environment, was able to accommodate these requests, often at short notice. In the 1970s we acknowledged radical changes in all the arts but we also recognised it was essential to accommodate artists involved in a more traditional language. We were equally determined to offer studio facilities and exhibition spaces to enable Welsh creatives to remain in Wales. The development of Chapter reflects cultural and sociological changes and exemplifies the way the arts have had to struggle for survival against depleted financial support and increasing institutional bureaucracy over the years. The success of Chapter has been due to committed teams of people who have believed in the value of an inclusive cultural organisation that welcomes all people, without exception.

In 1975, Bryan and I recognised Chapter needed a different management and renewed energy to take it forward into a new era. I had first talked to Paul Chandler in 1973 when he worked at the Royal Court Theatre, London and had contacted us about hosting a performance of *Sizwe Bansi is Dead*. Because of our conversations, I knew Paul was the person to take Chapter on to the next stage. He had been a founder of the Birmingham Arts Lab and had moved into other arts administrative roles. We succeeded in persuading

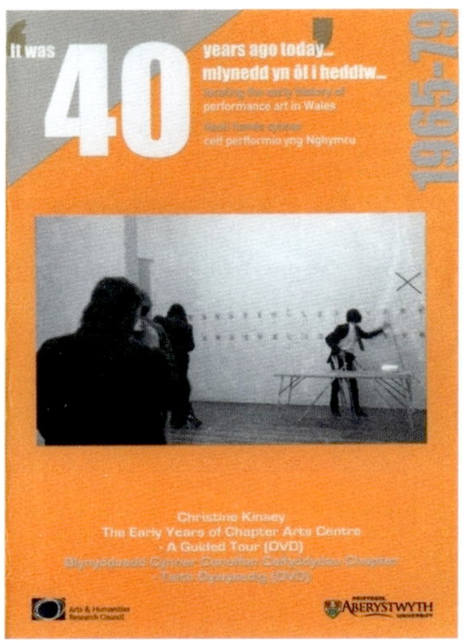

Three Art Centres Report, Arts Council of Great Britain 1975 Video interview with Christine Kinsey 40 years ago today – Heike Roms ©

him to come and work in Chapter, and it was his creative knowledge and empathy, together with his financial expertise, which established a stable administrative and financial structure that has allowed Chapter to continue to thrive. For over five decades, Chapter has grown into one of the largest arts complexes in Europe, with a major gallery and exhibition spaces, two cinemas, two theatres, a large number studios for performance and visual artists as well as creative industry offices, workshop spaces and meeting places for the community and a café bar. Chapter supports the production and presentation of the best national and international contemporary visual art, experimental and thought-provoking performance, and challenging independent, mainstream and international films, all alongside an inclusive learning programme that caters for all ages.

We had the support of many people I have not been able to mention and there have been multiple changes over the years, but for me Chapter has exceeded my wildest dreams. Essential for Chapter's continuing success is its support for professional artists of all disciplines living and working in Wales alongside promoting work by artists from other cultures, and keeping open lines of communication to creatively support society as a whole. The evolution of Chapter as a catalyst for the arts in Wales is based on the ethos of creative people working together with a common goal, namely, to produce the highest quality art and make it available both nationally and internationally to as wide an audience as possible, to explore and expand our understanding of the creative process and to respond to changing social expectations. Chapter celebrated its 50th anniversary in 2021, sadly, without Bryan and Mik but I know they would feel enormous pride and pleasure, like myself, that Chapter is still a very successful arts organisation, welcoming 800,000 people in 2019. Chapter Arts Centre has been many things to many people over the 50 years; my memories from the time are very personal, in that sense this is a selected history of Chapter. If in any way my recollections do not include everyone that was involved, you are invited by the team in Chapter to contribute your own memories to the archive.

I knew leaving Chapter and staying in Cardiff was going to be impossible for me. In fact, when people asked me if I had children my first thought was 'No, I had Chapter'. I did feel that by leaving I was losing my family, because the Chapter community had been my whole life. I decided to make a complete break in September 1976 by starting a new adventure on the island of Sint Maarten, in the Netherland Antilles, and return to my work as a visual artist.

1. Ken Baynes, *Art in Society* (London: Lund Humphries,1975), p.286.
2. Jon Gower, *Encounters with Karl Francis* (Swansea: H'mm Foundation, 2019).

Note: All designs for publicity are by Christine Kinsey or Bryan Jones unless otherwise stated. All photographs have been taken by Bryan Jones or Mik Flood unless otherwise stated.

Theatre – Elaine Mitchener
The Rolling Calf EXPERIMENTA
Photo: Kirsten McTernan

Gallery – Joy Labinjo
– kind permission of
Chapter Arts Centre

Cinema 2

Cardiff Animation Film Festival 2022, Cinema 1
Photo: Chris James

Theatre – Rhodri Davies & Lina Lapelyté, EXPERIMENTA
Photo: Warren Orchard

Chapter Light Box – Artist Carrie Mae Weems. Photo: Polly Thomas

Chapter Bar and Café
– Artist Carrie Mae Weems
Photo: Christine Kinsey

Alibis ***Crossing Borders***

*Left to myself, the dislocated memories constantly tug at censored choices
and compete to erode the ground that opens up an alternative time
when love was denied and lies became alibis, that spun around our split identity,
forsaking the truth changed the borders we crossed and recrossed
at the centre of inevitable loss.*

3

Myfyrdodau Caribïaidd

Caribbean Reflections

Taith y Pererin wrth Baentio a Darlunio

A Pilgrim's Progress in Painting and Drawing

Blodau'r Pabi / Poppies – *olew ar gynfas / oil on canvas 76 x 74 cm*

Arriving on the island of Sint Maarten, which is part of the Netherlands Antilles, at the end of August 1976 I was greeted by the news that La Grande Soufrière, a volcano on the neighbouring island of Guadeloupe, had erupted and a tidal wave and severe storms were expected. My reason for being on Sint Maarten was that I had been appointed to develop an arts programme in the school for professional and vocational training on the island, which was funded by a Dutch Foundation. Having made the decision to leave Chapter and seeing the advertisement in an educational journal, I applied for the job and was invited to a meeting in London with the Minister for Education and other government officials, at this point I thought I should find out the location of the island and discovered on a visit to Cardiff Library – Sint Maarten was in the Caribbean! and much to my surprise they offered me a three-year contract. It was certainly a step into the unknown and not an easy decision to make. I'm not quite sure how or what made me decide to go, but arriving in the aftermath of a volcanic eruption was not quite what I expected as my introduction to the life on the island, and made me wonder whether I had made the right decision. The drive from the airport to my hotel was eerie. It seemed that the island was in lock-down, waiting for the threatened devastating weather; my hotel in Philipsburg, the largest town on the island, had been boarded up against the onslaught. Some members of the newly appointed group of teachers had already arrived, including those who had been at the meeting in London, and some had come from Canada, the USA and other Caribbean islands. These teachers had been recruited to work in schools at all levels with a view to transferring the medium of education from Dutch to English, although the method of achieving this, especially for the junior school teachers, was not at all clear, as the Breakthrough Literacy scheme that had been planned was inexplicably abandoned just before we arrived.

The following day the weather exploded, with fierce winds driving horizontal rain and tremendous waves onto our hotel. We were constantly assured, however, this weather would not last and if it became too dangerous, we would be evacuated to higher ground, as patients and staff at the hospital had been previously. We were marooned for two weeks, and some teachers with families became so anxious they left the island and didn't return. During this time I learned that in the past Sint Maarten and Saint Martin, the French side of the island, had been colonised at different times by the Spanish, French and Dutch. These periods of colonisation had eliminated indigenous Arawak and Carib Amerindians, originally from South America, and their traditional society and deities. In 1493, on his second voyage to the West Indies, Christopher Columbus had claimed the island for Spain and called it Isla de San Martin. It was the French and Dutch who eventually split the 34-square-mile island between them, the French claiming a large area in the north, and the

Gwagedd / Vanity – *ysgrythiad / etching 42.5 x 29.7 cm*

Dutch a smaller area in the south, with valuable salt ponds. The two regions were separated by a border which crossed the range of hills that form a spine from north to south, both the French and Dutch economies had been at their most profitable when the slave trade was at its height. Although slavery was abolished in the 1800s, the trauma of this history still casts a long shadow, not only over this island but over the whole of the Caribbean.

At the end of those first two weeks I was introduced to some members of staff at the Foundation School, which had been set up by two Dutch businessmen to offer a secondary school education in English to all students, from every community and background. The only other secondary school taught all subjects in Dutch, as did the infants and junior schools, which meant that pupils up to the age of seventeen were taught in Dutch but spoke English in their daily life. The Dutch language was perceived as limiting young people's chances of moving on either to higher education or employment in the dominant tourist industry. The small number of classrooms at the Foundation School had been built out of concrete blocks with holes for windows and storm shutters which were needed in the hurricane season. On enquiring about the art room, I was given a jam jar with six worn-out brushes and shown a large tamarind tree in the fenced-off grounds. With a week before the students were to arrive, I had to work fast to gather enough materials to begin to develop a syllabus to teach art and design. I contacted the headmaster of the established junior school in Philipsburg and we struck a bargain: he would give me some art materials if I agreed to teach an art class in his school. In the first year at the Foundation School there was no art room and I moved from one classroom to another with materials that fitted into a shopping bag; even so, the understanding and enthusiasm of the young people I worked with constantly amazed me, as often it was the first time they could explore their world through creativity. By the end of the first school year, enough money had been raised to build a workshop and art room as part of the Foundation School complex and when the students returned at the

Gobaith / Hope – ysgrythiad / etching 42.5 x 29.7 cm

beginning of my second year, in September 1977, the art room had chairs, tables and some art materials.

The original ethos of the Foundation School was laudable, but it was corrupted by the English colonialist, white-racist attitude of the headmaster, who had previously taught at a private school in Barbados. He was appointed halfway through my first year and manipulated the school to serve white, middle-class children who only made up one per cent of all students. The school had been set up as a free school, but the headmaster, with his private school background, persuaded the founders to charge pupils and despite protests from many teachers, including myself, the school became fee-paying. Some of the children were from English-speaking islands and many were brought up by their mothers, sometimes in extended female families, but almost invariably with absent fathers. Many of these children lived in one-storey, single-room, basic concrete houses or wooden shacks, where whole families shared the space and sometimes slept in shifts. Although better-off families cooked on stoves with bottled gas, poorer families cooked outside on primitive pottery stoves that used charcoal, known as *coal pots*, and often had to walk some distance to get water from a well. If there was no cistern to collect rainwater in the hurricane season, the main way of bathing was taking a *sea bath*. Many mothers were exploited and employed to do the most menial work on extremely low wages, therefore, paying for one child or more to go to school was extremely difficult. I knew of girls in their teens who were working as prostitutes in Philipsburg, where men, mostly older and white, paid them for sex, and some pupils sold drugs to pay their school fee

Over the following years, using money from my salary and fundraising, I managed to support some children who otherwise would have had to leave school. The school became a very difficult place to work because of the division between teachers who advocated a private, fee-paying system, and the others who were determined to keep the original

Yr Ymadawiad / The Passing
– *dyfrlliw ar bapur / watercolour on paper 84.1 x 59.4 cm*

philosophy of the school: free to all who wanted an education. Despite these difficult circumstances, there were some great successes. Two of my year one pupils designed a poster which they said represented their friendship. The girls painted and drew their own hands and created a design showing black hands and white hands intertwined in a circle; this won a poster competition and represented the Caribbean during the International Year of the Child in 1979. It was a landmark event for all children, parents and teachers on Sint Maarten. The morning I announced to year one that the girls' poster had won, a pupil remarked, 'You know, Miss, I really didn't try my best when you asked us to enter this competition; I thought because we are black and we live on a tiny island, no-one would take any notice of us'. This comment echoed the feelings of many of the young people on the island who were of Amerindian, African, Indian and Asian descent and whose families were still being oppressed by colonialism, this time American. The islands' history of slavery was still very evident. Sint Eustatius, one of three islands in the northern Netherlands Antilles, had been a major trading station during the seventeenth and eighteenth centuries; this included a slave market where two thousand to three thousand Afro-Caribbean slaves were bred, stored and auctioned at any one time on its 8.1 square miles. Women and men were treated as 'reproductive livestock' and children as 'commodities' to be sold for the highest price. Sint Eustatius, which could be seen from Sint Maarten, was a clear historical reminder for young people of a colonialist past. They needed to be convinced their 'lives mattered' and were as important as any other child, anywhere in the world.

For the majority of students on Sint Maarten moving on to higher education was just a dream, made even more difficult, at the Foundation School, by the Cambridge O level exam system imposed by the headmaster. One of my fourth year students had to face this obstacle. He had left school in St Kitts and decided, with the support of his family, to come to the Foundation School when he was seventeen, in order to apply to Jamaica School of Art for a place on a course in Graphic Design and Illustration. For this he needed to have an art qualification and submit a portfolio. Working extremely hard, he produced highly skilled work for his portfolio, but taking the Cambridge O level examination was another matter. The illustration question asked the student to produce images based on two poems. The first poem was about a vicar on his bicycle riding through country lanes in England, looking at daffodils and listening to blackbirds; the second poem was about a train gushing out steam in a railway station covered in snow and ice in Moscow. Both of these scenes were outside his experience, he had never been to England, been on a train nor encountered ice and snow. At that time, in 1978, the only available information resource was a small library in Philipsburg which housed mostly Dutch-language books

Front St, Sint Maarten
– ysgrythiad / etching 42.5 x 29.7

and a limited range of American literature. But, even so, he still managed, through great determination, to gain the required O level and was accepted into the Jamaica School of Art where he gained a Diploma in Art and Design. This was the first person from his family to go on to higher education and the first person from Sint Maarten to go to art school. He returned to Sint Maarten to set up a design company and teach art and design at the Foundation School.

The deal I brokered with the headmaster of Philipsburg Junior School for art materials was that I would work with a group of teenage boys who were still in junior school because they hadn't gained the standard of education to go to secondary school. The teaching conditions in this school, as in most schools, were far from ideal. The art room was an old wooden building that had been the original school; it was open to the elements and to all the people walking past on Front Street, which meant that my class sometimes had an audience from the enormous cruise ships which docked in Philipsburg harbour. The group of teenage boys had a reputation of being 'bad boys' who couldn't read or write. Some of them had been expelled from school on the French side of the island where they been taught in French but lived in English, others had come from English-speaking islands. Their families, if they wished to stay and work on Sint Maarten, were obliged to send their children to school; these boys didn't want to be in school and, when told they had to take art and craft, they were not impressed. How was I going to get their attention? Thinking of some wonderful rebellious pupils I'd worked with successfully in

Menyw o Dristwch / Woman of Sorrows – *gouache ar bapur / gouache on paper 84.1 x 59.4 cm*

Wedi Canfod Menyw Coll 1 / Lost Woman Found 1 – *olew ar gynfas / oil on canvas 100 x 100 cm*

the past, I decided to use the same approach by giving them choices within a particular theme. The theme would be the music of Bob Marley and they were asked to design and make a record cover based on their favourite song; we listened to his *Natty Dread* album and their favourite track – also mine – was 'No Woman, No Cry'. The boys worked for weeks, listening to the music, making art and discussing the impact of Bob Marley on the Caribbean. They each designed and made their record cover with pencils, paint and collage and were so impressed with what they had achieved they wanted to carry on. I raised $100 from the owner of a large hotel on the island, and used it to buy sheets of plywood, saws and glue. Each boy made a rack to hold the record covers, with a wooden fretwork image on either end – fretwork being a local skill used to decorate the wooden houses. At the end of the year we held an exhibition which attracted many visitors and at the close we celebrated with a feast of jerk chicken. On Sint Maarten I used my married name, Jones, which I had never done before and the morning class would often start with the boys serenading me with 'Me and Mrs Jones, we have a (art) thing going on' from the Billy Paul song. Working with these boys was one of the most enjoyable times in all my teaching career.

Bryan left Chapter in 1977, to come to Sint Maarten, where he would return to painting. A short time after his arrival he was commissioned to produce a painting of one of the luxurious second homes built by wealthy Americans, who had taken over the most beautiful areas along the coast and lagoon. This painting was a great success and he was commissioned to paint many more. It was only then we were made aware of the grandeur of some of the mansions, owned by well-known American celebrities from the arts, business, and politics, hidden behind walls and electric fencing, protected by dogs and security guards. I attempted to raise money from some of these people to support children going to school but the majority showed a complete lack of interest in improving educational opportunities for young people living on the island. As Bryan's success grew, he rented a studio and was represented by an agent who promoted his paintings and with whom he designed some of the earliest Designer Sneakers. The first design specifically for children was called the *Explorer Sneaker*, to which cartoon characters were added when they were manufactured in Taiwan and sold initially in the American Midwest. Bryan saw his success as a means to an end and through his design work and sale of paintings he was able to support the work I was doing within the educational system and, in this way, we enabled more children to go to school.

Sint Maarten is a tax-free island; during the 1970s a delegation was set up by the Dutch authorities to investigate claims of corruption in the government on the island and

Cyfiawnder / Justice – *ysgrythiad / etching* 42.5 x 29.7 cm

its links to organised crime, money laundering and, later, syndicates supporting Islamic extremists, smuggling cocaine and emeralds, as well as trafficking women and girls from South America. The plight of many women and girls in the Caribbean is shocking. Sint Maarten boasted two brothels: the Seaman's Club and the Japanese Club, and it was no secret that young women and girls were being transported through the ports to America and into prostitution and slavery. On my first visit home to Wales I saw a short report in a national newspaper about a ship's container being found on the dock in Philipsburg, on its way to the United States, with 25 women and girls inside; 11 of them had died of suffocation. On my return to Sint Maarten I asked questions about the report and was told that no-one knew anything about it and if I wanted to remain on the island my questions should stop. Although I persisted there was no satisfactory answer. The lives of many women in the Caribbean continue to be fraught with danger because of corrupt cartels, usually ignored by governments. At the time, women in Dominica were being used as guinea pigs for a 'long-lasting contraception' experiment and on many islands Nestlé exploited women, who lived in poverty and struggled to survive, by aggressively marketing a 'dried milk formula', offering free samples to persuade mothers to change from breastfeeding to bottle feeding their babies. With no access to clean water nor any means of sterilising bottles the tragic aftermath of this scandal was that babies died.

Slavery and the lack of reparation by slave owners including Royal families, members of governments and the church continue to affect the development of generations of people who are subjugated to corrupt governments and multinational companies. It was hoped that Grenada would be an exception when Grenadian lawyer Maurice Bishop, who had studied at the University of London, returned to the island in 1970 and attempted to advocate change. He became the leader of the New Jewel Movement which included the remarkable woman Jacqueline Creft as the Minister of Education. This Movement sought

Callindeb / Wisdom – *ysgrythiad* / *etching 42.5 x 29.7 cm*

to affirm the need for social, economic and educational development as well as Black Liberation that had grown throughout the 1960's. There was a belief, by some politically motivated and educated young people that slavery was genocide, because of the systematic way slaves were tyrannised, persecuted and abused by a system which took the wealth out of the islands and left a legacy of poverty, illiteracy, racial degradation and ill health. During March 1979 the Leaders of the Jewel Movement replaced the Prime Minister Eric Gairy, who was accused of numerous human-rights abuses being perpetrated by his private army known as the Mongoose Gang, which terrorised his opponents. A priority for the New Jewel Movement was to build an international airport which was being supported by Cuba, this was viewed as threatening by the American Government. The situation on Grenada deteriorated because of the various factions vying for control and Maurice Bishop was put under house arrest. On October 19th 1983 a group of supporters released him and they all made their way to the miliary compound at Fort Rupert. Maurice Bishop, Jacqueline Creft, three other cabinet members and members of the Labour Movement were captured by troops, at the behest of the Deputy Prime Minister Bernard Coard and under the command of General Hudson Austin they were lined up against a wall and shot. Within six days Ronald Reagan sent American troops to invade the island on the pretext that they were rescuing American students from the St George's University Medical School. The Point Salines International Airport was completed with American support in 1984 and renamed the Maurice Bishop International Airport in 2009.

My three-year contract at the Foundation School ended in 1979 and was not renewed, neither were the contracts of other teachers who had tried to keep the school non-fee-paying for the majority of children. Pupils and their parents protested about the loss of teachers and organised a meeting to try and reverse the decision, but with no success. Despite my contract not being renewed, I decided to remain on Sint Maarten for another year to work with students who needed help with their exams and to spend more time on the nearby island of Nevis, which had become a special place for me. The islands of St Kitts and Nevis are affiliated and form the smallest sovereign state in the western hemisphere. On my first visit, I travelled to Nevis on a ferry boat from St Kitts and was unnerved to see soldiers with combat rifles patrolling the boat. I was told this was because of drug smuggling but later learned the reason was much more complicated. Nevis was very different to Sint Maarten, as the blight of tourism had not infected the island. There was a sense of belonging and that people understood where they had come from and who they were, within a distinct culture they had preserved. During this visit I met two remarkable women, Miss Maud Crosse and her cousin, known as Aunt Lynne, who had been teachers and lived in the capital, Charlestown. Miss Maud had been the headmistress of the Anglican infant and junior school and was politically active. She wanted to protect Nevis from the domination of St Kitts over the island's social and cultural structure, as well as its educational policy. Miss Maud knew she was on the 'A-list' of political troublemakers because she spoke out against the unjust political policies of the government of St Kitts, and the under-funding of public services on Nevis. She told me the soldiers stationed on the boat were put there by the government of St Kitts in order to

Calon Mas / Heart of Mas – *gouache ar bapur / gouache on paper 84.1 x 59.4 cm*

intimidate people on Nevis and discourage them from retaliating.

Nevis had been inhabited by Amerindians until the fifteenth century, when it was conquered by the Spanish and later by the British, who owned plantations growing sugar and cotton, creating enormous wealth for just a few landowners. The plantation workers were mainly slaves of African descent and in some cases had been 'imported' from Sint Eustatius. Miss Maud and Aunt Lynne were descendants of slaves who had worked in plantations which had become derelict; some of these had been turned into luxury hotels accessible only to very wealthy clients. After more than three hundred years of English, then British, colonial rule, St Kitts and Nevis became independent on 19th September 1983. Nevis had been particularly disadvantaged throughout this period because of receiving minimal financial support for infrastructure and public amenities, including a hospital. However, the dedication and determination of teachers developed a school system that provided some of the highest standards of junior and secondary education in the Caribbean. The first nursery school opened in the early 1970s when Miss Maud and Aunt Lynne financially supported building the school and sending students to be trained, as teachers, in Barbados.

Rhyddid / Freedom – *pensil ar bapur / pencil on paper 42.5 x 29.7 cm*

Miss Maud had also been working to set up a crafts co-operative in the belief that the pitfalls and dangers of basing the economy on tourism, as had happened on Sint Maarten, could be avoided by developing a sustainable creative industry. Cotton growing had recently been reintroduced onto the island with financial help from the Canadian Government. I was asked to organise screen-printing workshops, as Miss Maud was planning to harvest the cotton crop in order to spin, weave and print fabric to make garments which would be sold through outlets on other islands. Making Pottery was a skill which had been handed down from women who had been brought from Africa as slaves and continued as a tradition among women in the Newcastle area. I was introduced to two of the women potters, Mrs Jones and Veronica, and was able to see how they produced

Masquerade – *gouache ar bapur / gouache on paper 51 x 40 cm*

Mari Lwyd – *olew ar gynfas / oil on canvas 51 x 40 cm*

pottery, ranging from small bowls to three-foot-high pots, used to keep water cool in the heat. The clay was brought down from the mountain, by men loading it onto donkeys that were guided down to the village, where the clay was cut into blocks and stacked ready to be used. The clay needed to be sieved to remove all the stones, by the women who sat with their legs on either side of long stools; it was then kneaded and rolled into strands which they coiled to build their pots. Using a cloth inside and a stick outside, the pot was smoothed to form the surface, which was burnished with a stone to make it non-porous. Mrs Jones said her stone had been handed down through generations of women in her family who had been slaves brought from west Africa. I was amazed the first time I saw Mrs Jones and Veronica fire their pots, they laid them in a shallow pit on a bed of coconuts which had been split in half, covered them with palm leaves and set them alight, remarkably not one pot was damaged when they were taken out. To enable the women potters to develop their pottery, Miss Maud commissioned an American potter to introduce the Raku process, which was empathetic to their traditional method of working.

The major cultural event on Nevis is Culturama, which began in 1974. Slaves were emancipated on 1st August 1834 and on this day each year the freeing of slaves is remembered and celebrated. During this event African and European cultures interweave. The masquerade is based on the story of Giant Despair from *The Pilgrim's Progress* by John Bunyan, but interspersed with words and rituals from African traditions. The heroes Christian and Hopeful are captured and imprisoned in Doubting Castle. The narrative continues with Christian's journey to Celestial City and concludes with the death of Giant Despair. It is a great honour to play Christian and the role is handed down from father to son. The main characters are accompanied by Moko Jumbies, played by men and women on high stilts, as well as men dressed as women dancing to the rhythm of a *string band* that includes banjo, guitars and improvised instruments, mainly percussion. All the characters have painted faces and are dressed in costumes of brightly coloured material, often with very large straw masks decorated with peacock feathers. These costumes and traditions are a tribute to the West African culture that slaves brought to Nevis, which has been proudly resurrected and still flourishes. Another ceremony is when a costumed figure leads a character wearing the tiger's head and follows the parade, chasing the children in the crowd and goes from house to house calling to the residents who are expected to respond in kind, it reminded me of the Welsh folk tradition of the *Mari Lwyd* where a character wears a horse's head and is led by a costumed figure. The origins of this tradition on Nevis was *Cariso* which was sung and chanted by *Chantwells*, who were mostly female slaves, they used call-and-response chants to preserve the complex oral tradition of West Africa. It was a way of communicating with other enslaved Africans who were

Painting workshops Charles Town, Nevis

Masquerade – Painting for the Library, Charles Town, Nevis – *acrylig ar fwrdd / acrylic on board 2.43 m. x 1.2 m*

Y Sgarff Goch / The Red Scarf
– *olew ar gynfas / oil on canvas*
50 x 30 cm

stripped of all connections to their home, land and family and were not allowed to speak to each other. Calypso grew out of Cariso and continues to play an important role in Culturama, when Calypsonians often include lyrics in their songs to protest against colonial rule, political corruption, poor economic situations and discrimination, which they would not be able to vocalize in any other way.

In 1985 I returned to Nevis while I was working on a series of gouache paintings, drawings and etchings for my exhibition *A Pilgrim's Progress in Painting and Drawing*. While planning this work I contacted the people in Cardiff who had worked with me on the exhibition called *Carnival* in the gallery at Chapter This resulted in an Arts Council of Wales commission to work with young people to celebrate the strong connections between Wales and the Caribbean. One of the developments of this project resulted in working with Miss Maud and organising workshops with both Nevisian adults and children, which resulted in a very large painting on board called *Culturama*. It shows the mixture of traditions and culture that were part of the identity of Nevis and now hangs in the Charlestown library.

Bryan returned to our house in Cardiff in the Autumn of 1980, and after organising an exhibition of paintings and drawings from our time in the Caribbean, in a gallery on Long Island, New York, I joined him in January 1981. Returning from the Caribbean I was not expecting to be confronted with the shameful racism and discrimination that continued to exist in Britain. This became apparent soon after I had returned, when driving past the Civic Centre in Cardiff I saw a young black woman standing on the side of the road with two cases on the ground next to her; I stopped and asked if there was a problem. She had enrolled on a degree course at the University of Wales in Cardiff and had arrived from London to stay in bed and breakfast accommodation. When she arrived at the house a woman had opened the door and said 'Sorry love we don't take blacks, it's not me it's my husband' and closed the door. It was shocking to me that this could happen, especially in Cardiff, with a multi-heritage history that is crucially important to Wales. I invited the young woman, Brenda, to come and stay at our house while I found out why the University of Wales had not offered accommodation to a first-year student, and what they were going to do about it. Brenda stayed with us until the University found her a place to live in a safe environment. The Black Lives Matter movement is continuing the fight for equality and justice for people from multi-heritage backgrounds. Following the Hidden Heroines campaign organised by Monumental Welsh Women in Wales, a statue of Betty Campbell, Wales' first black Headteacher and a champion of multiculturalism was commissioned and erected, during 2021, in Cardiff; could this recognition mean that, at last, things are changing for women and the multi-heritage communities?

In September 1982 Bryan and I moved to a house with no electricity and in need of complete renovation in a beautiful rural area of the Teifi valley. In sharp contrast to the weather we had left in the Caribbean, that winter was one of the harshest on record, and on 8th January Wales was in the grip of one of the worst blizzards of the twentieth century. The country lanes filled with snow and the only way into the cottage was to climb in through a high window. But it was a very happy time; we used Tilley lamps and cooked on an open fire which also kept us warm and the whole house from freezing. On excursions to farms across the fields to collect potatoes, onions and any other vegetables they could spare, we made friends with the most wonderful neighbours. Spring was late, but when it came the garden began to reveal its secrets, and seeing the first snowdrops emerge is still a precious memory.

As soon as we moved into our house Bryan and I began the restoration and set up studios. I had produced some drawings and paintings while on Sint Maarten, but coming home to Wales I needed to work back through the enigma that the Caribbean islands had been for me. Working with Nevisians made me realise how important it had been for them to find a way of preserving their cultural heritage and making it relevant to young people in order to establish a positive way forward. In many ways I recognised similarities with Wales and the preservation of our language and culture. I did not want to be a bystander in another culture and my exile in the Caribbean reinforced that to work as an artist I needed to be in my own country: Wales.

Developing the images for *A Pilgrim's Progress in Painting and Drawing* was in part an attempt to understand why I needed to return to where my life had begun: growing up in the industrial valleys of south east Wales. My quest was to understand my identity as a woman within the culture of Wales and so it was necessary for me to develop a visual language that revealed Cymreictod – feeling / being Welsh.

Yr Ymweliad / The Visit – *olew ar gynfas / oil on canvas 100 x 100 cm*

Alibis ***Aberfan Disaster 9-15 a.m. Friday, 21st October, 1966***

As the rain pours each day into the next, waste from the bowels of the Earth slithers its way towards the school slurping over the protective wall, pushing on it climbs to the window and peers in, children and teacher unaware of its gaze until the dark extinguishes the light, then the violated history of their land gathers its subjects in a suffocating embrace, taking its fill it leaves and squeezes out through the door down the steps to the road, ignorant of left or right, at the playing field it stops; as the only absent boy holds up his hand.

4

Hunaniaeth a Pherthyn | Identity and Belonging

Cymreictod Menywod Cymru

Women of Wales

Living in the Caribbean for four years had reinforced my sense of Cymreictod – an innate feeling of being Welsh – and also my need to live and work in Wales. It had been a time of reflection and a recognition of how important the culture of Wales is to my identity and creativity, which are rooted in growing up in the industrial valleys of south Wales. The visual culture of Wales has often been undervalued. In his book *The History of Wales* John Davies states that, in comparison to other forms of creativity in Wales: 'There is less to be said about the visual arts.'[1] However, he offers no justification for this statement. I would suggest this misconception has been perpetrated historically because the diversity of the visual art of Wales has not been fully acknowledged nor represented in public galleries and museums. Consequently, Wales has been perceived as a nation without a strong visual tradition. For decades the Art Galleries at National Museum Cardiff were reluctant to develop their collections to include art produced in Wales by Welsh artists, not least women artists. Exhibitions such as the *British Art Show* and *Artes Mundi* have included very few artists – and even fewer women artists – from Wales. Generally, women are under-represented in Welsh public art collections, which means fewer visible role models for emerging female artists.

This was highlighted, for me, by an incident related by Miss Eluned Jones, who had been the dedicated and inspiring headmistress of Cardiff High School for Girls for twenty years. In the early 1970s, Miss Jones supervised the amalgamation of Cardiff High School for Girls into the comprehensive system and when this was nearing completion she paid a final visit to her old school. There, to her dismay, she found some of the portraits of headmistresses since the school first opened in 1895, stacked against a skip ready to be thrown away. Miss Jones only just managed to save them. The portraits included one of Miss Mary Collin, the first headmistress, 1895-1924; she had been a leading suffrage campaigner and continued to work for women's rights into her old age. Fortunately, the oil pastel portrait of *Mary Collin* by Mrs C. Blakeney Ward (1924) is now in the national collection at St Fagans National Museum of History.

These portraits represent a highly significant part of the history of representing women's achievements in Wales, and this story demonstrates a profound lack of understanding by public authorities regarding the importance of portraiture in relation to our inherited visual language and also our social history. In recent years there has, at last, been a growing awareness concerning the importance of portraits found in libraries, chapels and other public buildings; some have been identified and preserved, but much still needs to be done. While working on my exhibition *Cymreictod – Menywod Cymru / Women of Wales* between 1985 and 1989, I became increasingly conscious of the lack of

Heb Lais / Without a Voice
– *olew ar gynfas / oil on canvas 204 x 122 cm*

Y Chwiorydd Gregynog / The Gregynog Sisters – *siarcol / pensil ar bapur / charcoal / pencil on paper 84.1 x 59.4*

portraits of women and named women artists in some Welsh national institutions. For this reason, I asked the galleries and museums where my exhibition was to be shown to organise a 'sister' exhibition of portraits either of women or by women from their collections to underline not only the importance of portraiture but also the role women had played in the arts and society.

Newport College of Art in the early 1960s was a typical male-dominated environment, as were many other colleges of art, where women were mostly ignored and made to feel invisible, just as they were in the wider art world. Women were learning more about being liberated from the traditional limitations on their lives in books by Simone de Beauvoir and Betty Friedan. In 1962, as an art student, I became aware of the concept of *feminism* for the first time; it was exciting to read about women's sexual and personal freedom. Male tutors and students ridiculed and dismissed these ideas, using words like *feminist* and *women's lib* as derogatory terms. The second-wave feminist movement was gaining ground throughout the 1960s and into the 1970s and was reflected in the writing of Welsh women.

Elaine Morgan was born in Hopkinstown and lived in Mountain Ash, both in Rhondda Cynon Taf. for most of her life. After studying at Oxford University she became a successful journalist and writer for television. Her pioneering book *The Descent of Woman* describes the important role women played in human evolution and it became one of the principal antidotes to sexist theories that had become the accepted norm. Elaine Morgan's writing, supported by the feminist movement, opened the way for critics to label her books 'feminist science', undermining their validity and her research. *The Descent of Woman* became an international bestseller and for the following ten years she continued to research the aquatic ape hypothesis, producing *The Aquatic Ape* in 1982. Writing a further three books developing the same subject led her to conclude that the biblical Genesis myth which portrayed Eve as an afterthought to the creation of man was a device to

Cylch Bywyd 1 / Life Cycle 1 – *olew ar gynfas / oil on canvas 183 x 122 cm*

Cylch Bywyd 2 / Life Cycle 2 – *olew ar gynfas / oil on canvas 183 x 122 cm*

Cylch Bywyd 3 / Life Cycle 3 – *olew ar gynfas* / *oil on canvas 183 x 122 cm*

undermine the role of women in the evolution of humankind. This proposition caused great consternation in both religious and scientific communities. I had long admired her writing and was delighted when she agreed to accept my invitation to speak at a conference on Spiritual and Religious Experience at the Alister Hardy Religious Experience Research Centre, University of Wales, Lampeter. I visited her at home in Mountain Ash and it was a privilege to be able to talk with her over a period of time.

Other Welsh women authors continued to support the equal rights and the feminist movement in Wales. I was particularly struck by Deirdre Beddoe's statement in her book *Out of the Shadows: A History of Women in Twentieth-century Wales*: 'It can be argued too that Welsh women were subjected to a particularly "virulent strain" of patriarchy'.[2] Feminist writers led the way to establish women-only publishing companies as a vehicle to convey their message and reflect women's interests and concerns. Honno: Welsh Women's Press was established in 1986 by a group whose aim was to promote women writers and poets, past and present, in the Welsh and English languages, because they perceived the male-dominated publishing houses in Wales discriminated against women writers. Other publications, such as *Spare Rib*, the second-wave feminist magazine, consisted of new writing and was published between 1972 and 1993. Penny Simpson reviewed my exhibition *Cymreictod – Menywod Cymru / Women of Wales* in *Spare Rib* (Issue 211, August 1990). These publishers and writers challenged stereotyping and exploiting women while supporting solutions to the social and cultural problems they faced.

The seminal women writer's conference *Imagined Realities* organised by Sue Harries on behalf of Yr Academi Gymreig was held in Dyffryn House, St Nicholas, Cardiff in October 1982. The conference included Margaret Atwood, Beryl Bainbridge, Angela Carter, Ruth Fainlight, Emma Tennant, Eigra Lewis Roberts and Fay Weldon. Listening to these remarkable women talking about their writing, as I was planning to start to work my idea of *Cymreictod* in relation to *Menywod Cymru / Women of Wales*, has had a lifelong impact on my creativity. Sue Harries also arranged writing workshops for unemployed people in the South Wales Valleys called *Write About It*. Bryan and I designed the publicity and I led the workshops that were held in Pont-y-pool in Autumn 1982. It was inspiring to work with a group of very talented writers and poets who were writing about their personal experiences of growing up in the Blaenavon valley, 'living on the dole' and how it had changed their lives, in most cases for the worse. The writing workshops created a support for some people to move on to higher education, for example to Coleg Harlech.

The emerging feminist movement, and lack of opportunities for women in the arts, was in the forefront of my mind in the 1970s while I was setting up and organising events in Chapter. During this time we endeavoured to provide spaces for the production and presentation of work by all artists but recognised that women, including those with children, faced particular problems. We supported setting up a nursery school and crèche in Chapter, which was one way of involving children in an arts community as part of their day-to-day lives, and offering women an opportunity to work in studio spaces and become involved with the creative life in the building. Women were generally more reluctant to assert what they needed to enable them to be involved in the arts, and encouraging mothers to accompany their children when they came with school visits to see exhibitions, I hoped would overcome some of the preconception that the arts did not include them. Over a period of time many more women developed their work in the visual arts, theatre, film, video, music and performance, with Chapter providing spaces which supported new and innovative ideas

Cof / Memory Pont-y-moel
– *siarcol / pensil ar bapur / charcoal / pencil on paper 84.1 x 59.4*

Modernism was viewed by many artists in the 1960s, especially women, as elitist, white male-dominated, and disinterested in minorities. Postmodernism was welcomed by many feminist artists internationally who were outraged by their continuing ostracism from the dominant modernist tradition, in particular from painting and sculpture. The multimedia approach of Postmodernist art practice was seen as a potentially radical intervention into what is still a ubiquitous male culture. The National Eisteddfod of Wales is an example of how many women artists exhibiting in Y Lle Celf continue to work in a wide range of media, which is a testament to how the Postmodernist phenomenon continues to influence their work. Women's visual art organisations struggled to be seen and heard, with some groups succeeding despite the difficulties. South Glamorgan Women's Arts Association, also known as Permanent Waves, organised the first annual International Women's Art's Festival in 1986, stating that the Association is 'committed to addressing the isolation and exclusion experienced by women in the arts and the wider community'. The funding that enabled the organisation to employ a member of staff was withdrawn in 2011; the reason they were given was that 'in the 1980s when the Association began there was a clear need to support such an organisation but today this isn't the case' – a conclusion which shows a lack of understanding by funding bodies of the continuing

Marwnad / Elegy – *olew ar gynfas /*
oil on canvas 183 x 122 cm

difficulties faced by women in the arts. An organisation like this is, most definitely, still needed as most women working in all the arts know from experience, and the Association continues to provide support for women on a voluntary basis.

Exasperated by the marginalisation of work by women film-makers in an industry controlled by men, inside and outside Wales, a number of women in Chapter formed the South Wales Women's Film Group in November 1981, the first women's film organisation in Wales. The group's intention was to share skills, support ideas and enable women to play a more active role in film-making. Red Flannel Films, founded in 1986 by members of this group, told the story, through film, of the miner's strike in 1984-1985. The films represented women in the South Wales Valleys who had taken a lead in the miners' strike against pit closures. Chapter Video Workshop made a major contribution to the women's video movement and both groups supported film and video makers, as well as offering opportunities to younger women. The Workshop evolved by teaching countless others how to make, as well as present, film and video in an industry that embodied female discrimination.

The extraordinary Magdalena Project: An International Network of Women in Contemporary Theatre was first discussed by a group of women theatre-makers at a festival in Italy during 1983. Although the refurbishment of Chapter's theatre was not complete, the *Magdalena '86* festival was centred in and around Chapter and was the first international women in contemporary theatre festival in Wales. It was at this event that the Magdalena Project was founded in response to the lack of opportunity for women to represent themselves and have their own voice in theatre-making. This highly successful project has expanded to eight countries in South America as well as Australia, New Zealand, the USA, Singapore, India and Europe; these festivals give a platform for women to tell their stories creatively when it might otherwise be dangerous to do so or there are no other means possible. In 1999 the Arts Council of Wales

Eiliad yn y Ddawns / A Moment in the Dance – *olew ar gynfas / oil on canvas 36 x 46 cm*

withdrew their funding from the Magdalena Project; this misguided decision closed the infrastructure of the Cardiff base. It is tragic that this opportunity is no longer available to women in Wales, nor – I may add – in Britain.

In 1997 Archif Menywod Cymru / Women's Archive Wales was established at the then University of Glamorgan, Pontypridd, in order to encourage people to preserve archives relating to the history of Welsh women who come from all backgrounds and have contributed to industrial, rural, minority and LGBTQ+ communities in Wales. Since the late 1970s, books about the hidden history of women from Wales have been making many more lives visible; it is essential the momentum created by pioneers of the rights of women is built upon and this archive is supported to record the remarkable history of women's lives in Wales. For example, there is ceramic artist and writer Ann Pettitt from Llanpumsaint, Carmarthenshire, who in 1981 organised a protest march from Cardiff to Greenham Common in Berkshire where American cruise missiles had been sited since 1979. She was instrumental in setting up the Women's Peace Camp which remained there until 2000. Other peace camps were established between 1984 and 1985 in Porth, Rhondda and Llanishen in Cardiff, and also in Brawdy, Pembrokeshire, where I and other artists set up camp to create paintings of the surrounding landscape. My painting, entitled *Copa Pen Beri*, was sold to support the women's peace movement Women for Life on Earth. Archif Menywod Cymru / Women's Archive Wales continues to record and make visible Welsh women's lives and offers younger

WN / Welsh NOT – *olew ar bapur / oil on paper 84.1 x 59.7 cm*

generations of women the opportunity to show and tell their stories.

Cymreictod was in the forefront of my thoughts when I began making the paintings and drawings for *Menywod Cymru / Women of Wales* in 1988. I needed to explore my identity and place in the world through my art, which I realised could only be developed out of my own experience. The one thing I knew something about was growing up female in the industrial valleys of Monmouthshire, which at that time was not officially part of Wales or England; the designation was 'Wales and Monmouthshire' until it was incorporated into Wales in 1974. As I was growing up it made me feel I didn't belong to any country; I once asked my mother whether we were Welsh or English, she said: 'Neither, love, we're mongrels.' When I became aware that place names were in Welsh, there seemed to be a choice, so I decided, as a teenager, that I was Welsh. My wish to learn more about my country was frustrated by the lack of Welsh history taught at school: the history book we used had only one small chapter about Wales. In some areas of Monmouthshire speaking Welsh, or the idea of Welshness, was thought to be 'common' and there were some members of my family who 'aspired' to be English. Perhaps this attitude to the idea of being Welsh and the Welsh language was a legacy of the 'Welsh Not', the wooden block with 'WN' written on it, hung around children's necks to punish them for speaking Welsh in school, and the notorious parliamentary report on education in Wales, which came to be known as *Brad y Llyfrau Gleision / The Treachery of the Blue Books* because it denigrated both the people of Wales and the Welsh language. The report was published in 1847, during the lifetime of my great-grandmother Mary Ann Morgan and would have affected many of her 11 children, including my grandmother.

Eiliad yn y Ddawns / A Moment in the Dance – *olew ar fwrdd / oil on board 41 x 31 cm*

In the area the Teifi valley, where Maes-y-crugiau and the house and studios Bryan and I had moved into from Cardiff was situated, our neighbours in the farms on either side of us lived and worked in Welsh. It was my first experience of living in a Welsh-speaking community and it opened a way of being connected to aspects of the culture of Wales that had seemed distant and mysterious. My key to this other world has been learning Welsh, which has revealed a new way of seeing the world through the ancient and modern literature of Wales. I greatly admired the courage of Welsh-language activists who throughout the second half of the twentieth century were ready to face being arrested or

Jesse (detail) – *pensil ar bapur / pencil on paper 84.1 x 59.7 cm*

imprisoned in order to preserve Welsh as a living language for future generations, and there are very moving accounts by some women involved. Menna Elfyn's poetry, which has been a major influence on my work, describes being in prison in her bilingual collection of poignant poems *Cell Angel* (1996). Menna's memory of that time is recorded in Deirdre Beddoe's book *Out of the Shadows: A History of Women in Twentieth-century Wales:*

> A law breaking dreamer, I eventually went to prison myself as a language activist, but came out a feminist. Imprisonment brought home to me the existence of another silenced war, waged this time against women.[3]

I planned that the paintings and drawings for *Cymreictod – Menywod Cymru / Women of Wales* would be *about* the women as well as being portraits of them. My aim was to make visible the positive contribution of women I knew, from a wide range of backgrounds, had made to the society and culture of Wales. The 'Welsh Mam' had become a sentimental cliché that trapped women into the image of a strong matriarchal figure dominating the household from her kitchen. This image reduces her to a purely domestic role and restricts her financial independence, as she was forced to rely on the men in the family for their income to support herself and the family. This depiction undermines the reality of the difficult and unrelenting struggle many women suffered. The first drawing I made, as part of this exhibition, was about my favourite aunt Jesse from Blaendare Road, and the stories she told me. Jesse and her husband Alf emigrated to Australia, sailing in September

1913 she was pregnant, tragically the baby died on the crossing. They kept a post office in the Outback and raised two children, returning to Wales after the children had grown up. I treasured the comforting evenings spent in front of an open fire, with my grandmother in her rocking chair and my aunt making supper with left-over bread, hot milk and sugar.

Bryan's mother, Yskir Kate Price, was born in Rhymney, Monmouthshire in 1898. She was named after a visit her mother made to the river Usk, on a charabanc outing, while she was pregnant. Her mother enjoyed herself so much she decided to make up a name for her baby to remember the day. Yskir married Sylvanus Jones who worked as a 'face worker' in the McLaren Colliery, Abertyswg and during their early married years they lived in a 'one-up, one-down' cottage in White Row, Rhymney. It was owned by the Tredegar Iron and Coal Company and was a tied cottage; if the miner lost his job or his life in one of the pit disasters, the family lost their home. At that time Sylvanus was paid in tokens which were only redeemable in the company truck shop where prices were very high; this economic slavery was imposed on many people in the industrial areas of the South Wales Valleys. Yskir had seven children, five of them born in White Row; much of the cottage was damp and to cover up the problem, the walls were papered with newsprint and then a thicker paper which was painted. The paper was often stuck onto the wall with flour and water, which attracted black cockroaches known as *blackpats*, brought home on working clothes from the mines. During the day they hid in the crevices in the wall but Yskir said she could hear them scuttling around at night and were the bane of her life. The room upstairs was divided by a curtain, with Yskir and Sylvanus' bed on one side and two beds for the children on the other side, the boys sleeping top to toe in one bed and the girls sleeping in the other. The

Yskir – *gouache ar bapur / gouache on paper 84.1 x 59.7 cm*

Miss Rhymney Valley
– *gouache ar bapur /*
gouache on paper
84.1 x 59.7 cm

Gladys and Ceini – *siarcol / pensil ar bapur / charcoal / pencil on paper 59.7 x 84.1 cm*

kitchen downstairs had a *bosh* (sink) with a cold water tap and an open fire in a black-leaded grate which Yskir cooked on, making stew with 'six penn'orth o' pieces' – cheap offcuts of meat. She boiled water on the fire for Sylvanus and the boys to bathe in a tin bath when they returned from the colliery, in front of the fire in the winter but at other times outside. To care for the family, Yskir was the first to get up in the morning and the last to go to bed. The two older boys left school at twelve years of age and went to work with their father in the McLaren Colliery. The oldest sister, at fourteen years of age, went to work 'in service' for a wealthy family in London. After her return to Rhymney, during the second world war, she worked at the Royal Ordinance Factory, Glascoed which was one of the munitions filling factories, the chemicals she worked with turned her skin yellow, which also affected many of the other women doing the same work. Although the younger sisters passed the eleven-plus they were unable to go to Rhymney Grammar School because there was not enough money to buy their uniforms and books, so they left school and worked in local factories. Bryan was the only boy in the family to pass the eleven-plus, and as a scholarship boy he was able to go to the Grammar School and complete his A levels; he then worked in Ebbw Vale steelworks before being called up for National Service in the Army and, afterwards, enrolling in Newport College of Art.

When the family had grown from five to seven children, Sylvanus and Yskir moved to Field St, Rhymney, which was a few doors away from the house where poet Idris Davies had been born and lived; he too worked as a miner in the McLaren Colliery. The couple lived through the 1926 and 1936 strikes and the Second World War, but even after the unbelievable hardships Yskir had weathered, when I met her in 1962 she was compassionate, caring, patient and still the most quietly girlish, joyous person I knew. Whenever I would say, 'Come on, Mam, let's go', she would take off her pinny, have her

Megan a'i Mam / Megan and her Mother
– pastel / siarcol / pensil ar bapur / pastel / charcoal / pencil on paper 100 x 100 cm

everything she was asked to do and she insisted on letting her auburn hair grow just to 'annoy her mother'. I also painted women from an early Welsh tradition, in particular tales of the *Mabinogion*. I was particularly interested in Branwen, who was given in marriage to the king of Ireland; the story ends when she dies of a broken heart, apparently blaming herself for the tragic consequences, although they are caused by the actions of men. I wanted to give women, like Branwen whose circumstances resonate today, a voice and tell their stories.

My focus in this exhibition was to paint the stories of real women of all ages and backgrounds, who were not always recognised for their contribution to family, community and society, as well as to celebrate imaginary women who had grown out of fictional stories I had heard as part of the culture of Wales. I have developed some of the women in *Cymreictod – Menywod Cymru / Women of Wales* into a group of characters who continue to inhabit my paintings, drawings and film; they accompany me on my explorations of other worlds which I have created through my imagination to form my other, parallel life.

1. John Davies, *The History of Wales* (London: Penguin, 2007), p.633.
2. Deirdre Beddoe, *Out of the Shadows: A History of Women in Twentieth-century Wales*. (Cardiff: University of Wales Press, 2000), p.180.
3. Beddoe, *Out of the Shadows*, p.166.

Menyw ar Bedestal / Woman on a Pedestal – *olew ar gynfas / oil on canvas 204 x 122 cm*

Alibis ***The Red Kerchief***

Who was she then arched in the grey and black of falling bridges in a dislocated land,
diagonal she stands looking down and back, lit right from darkest left,
out of her past she merges fisted hand out stretched passing over the underlying cause,
kerchief in red, the harbinger of remorse is knotted in love,
blood like it encircles and encapsulates a death that pains the deepest depths:
who is she now in retrospect, the answer denied by questioning.

5

Pontio Amser a Lle

Bridging Time and Place

Bywyd Arall

Another Life

Y Bont / The Bridge
– olew ar gynfas / oil on canvas
60 x 35 cm

Transforming the women in the paintings and drawings, which I had produced for *Cymreictod – Menywod Cymru / Women of Wales* into the female characters who appeared in the series of images I produced for *Bywyd Arall / Another Life*, was a way of articulating visually the relationship between my interior and exterior life. These images were sometimes based on childhood remembrances of growing up in Pont-y-Moel and the dilemmas these experiences had created in my life as well as my identity within the culture of Wales. Creating these women characters and pictorial worlds for them to inhabit enabled me to explore imaginary and illusionary time and space, as well as, the past, present and future with the characters often portrayed in continuous representation. The women became guides and messengers traversing inner worlds, outer worlds and otherworldliness, allowing me to distance myself from myself and articulate my ideas through them. My aim in these paintings and drawings was to create a bridge which would lead from an unconscious to a conscious awareness and bring into being, through my imagination, unspoken thought and feelings. I recognised the process of creating the women characters, who would accompany me on this odyssey of self-discovery, was a necessary way of resolving personal, moral and spiritual dilemmas and that it would form a psychological visual memoir.

My visual language is born from a creative process that in most cases begins with a word, often a word in Welsh, which stimulates my imagination, that part of our creative being which is often misunderstood and mostly unexplored. For many people, to talk about the imagination is to say things are not 'true'. But the imagination is, perhaps, the most defining characteristic of what it is to be human; it facilitates the peeling away of conscious thought to connect us with a mostly unknown universe within, which we have barely begun to understand. The imagination facilitates our transcendence of the material world by engaging with our unconscious and connecting us with our deepest feelings; through visual language the invisible can be made visible. The way women have been portrayed pictorially, is mainly through the male imagination, in Western culture from the early Renaissance up to and throughout the Modernist period and continues to influence the perception of women and how we perceive ourselves. I think of my imagination as a mental workshop, aiding me to create images through a female/feminist imagination, which could change how women were portrayed in stereotypical roles.

Cartref – Dychweliad / Home – Return
– *olew ar gynfas / oil on canvas 183 x 122 cm*

Gwlad – Troad Allan / Land – Expulsion
– olew ar gynfas / oil on canvas
183 x 122 cm

Creating my paintings involves a great deal of preparation: numerous drawings, colour studies and notations. When an image begins to develop in my mind the process of drawing and writing down words, sometimes in the form of poems, in my drawing book/journal eliminates what is not needed; it's a form of précising information to capture the core idea. The title is important because it is the seed from which my imagination can grow, but as the work progresses the title becomes less important when my visual language takes precedence. The structure and composition of the image are created by incorporating the abstract qualities of point, line, plane, curve, mass, weight, and density, which transform into symbols, signs and colour, all of which need to be considered for the image to become 'complete' within itself. I often recall the words of artist, writer and poet David Jones as I begin to make the first drawings: he believed it is the abstract quality in any work of art, however hidden or devious, which determines the real worth of the work, whatever the subject matter. This abstract visual language 'alphabet' was taught by drawing and painting from the figure, before it was excluded from the teaching syllabus in favour of – often written – conceptual presentations in many art colleges in Wales, as well as other parts of Britain during the late 1960s and 1970s. The repercussions are that some of the students who graduated were not fully visually literate when they completed their course. They had been deprived of a crucial understanding of the basic language of visual art, which has resulted in this language being on the verge of becoming extinct, because these students, who are now teachers, do not have the knowledge to pass on to pupils.

Having studied at Newport College of Art in the final years of the influence of Modernism I had thought Postmodernism would be a positive force. I had totally supported the concept during the early 1970s when I was programming the gallery, theatre and cinema in Chapter because it was a way of dismantling the dominance of the elitist Modernist culture and making the arts more available to a wider range of people. At the time, Postmodernism was particularly welcomed by many women artists because they were able to move in areas of creativity that had not yet been dominated by men. But throughout the 1980s and 1990s I was greatly concerned by the influence on students by tutors that had their own personal Postmodernist agendas. I had become disillusioned with mainstream Postmodernism and how many younger artists succumbed once again to commercially motivated practice, with collectors buying art as an investment rather than for the creative value of the work. Postmodernism became a rejection of the aesthetic value of visual art and emphasised the

Yr Awen – The Muse – *pastel / siarcol / pensil ar bapur – pastel /charcoal / pencil on paper 100 x 60 cm*

the dark towards the light – a mantra that is interwoven into my life as well as my philosophy of painting.

The skill of *seeing* not just *looking* is the basis of developing, a visual memory and a visual language which, together with gathering information in my drawing book/journal, has become the genesis of the image whether painting in gouache or oil paint. Laying out the oil colours on a large glass palette is full of expectation. All the reds from scarlet lake to alizarin crimson and caput mortuum are in a line on the left side, blues from Prussian blue, ultramarine – made originally from ground lapis lazuli, the most precious and expensive paint during the Renaissance – to cobalt blue across the top, with yellow ochre, cadmium yellow deep, plus Naples yellow, as well as Old Holland violet grey, unbleached white and titanium white down the left side. I take enormous pleasure 'activating' the colour by kneading, folding and blending the pigment and oil with a palette knife; as the colours are manipulated they take on a life of their own and become a 'living' thing. When the composition of the picture begins to take shape, rhythm dominates my perception, the faces, bodies and limbs of my characters in movement or stillness reveal balance and counterbalance; seemingly vagrant mixtures of colours, lines and forms hesitate, grow restless and resume their adventures. Colours link shapes and forms, light and shadow reveal or disguise a physical and spiritual bond, I believe, we have with the world around us. It is always my intention that this rhythm be realised in my painting and drawing, from observation and through conception to the physical act of making marks. Often, when I'm surprised by some unintended effect of a particular combination of colours, forms or movement into or out of the picture plane, I revise my intention.

Pont-y-moel – *pastel / siarcol / pensil ar bapur – pastel /charcoal / pencil on paper 30 x 20 cm*

The preliminary drawings and studies, and the detailed planning are reassessed, maybe adjusted, amended, demoted or accentuated and large areas may be reworked. What has disappeared is not absent but forms the layers of 'remembrances' that at a later stage reveal levels of a visual palimpsest through a reworking of the painted surfaces. Fresh insights bring their own

Llateies – Y Kerchief Goch –
Messenger / The Red Kerchief
– *olew ar gyfnas / oil on canvas 52 x 41 cm*

obligations; surprise and discovery are important elements as the painting develops and re-adjustment is constant in a progressing work, each mark alters what has gone before. All must be appraised, the past altered by the present, the present is always fresh, unexpected and stimulating. For me, this process of visual thinking makes a living thing out of the painting. Finally something says to me 'this is real'. Then I stop. I find the planning, the process, the act of painting satisfies a need – I feel whole. My intention is that my paintings are not only a representation of the subject but the subject itself – not only a representation of an emotion but the emotion itself. The quintessential reason for my paintings to exist is they inhabit the universe, not just comment on it.

Creating this *other world* I can acknowledge *another self* and live *another life* in parallel to my existing life. Exploring concepts of the material and spiritual, in the *space between*, always seemed to be a place of immeasurable possibilities. Acting as guides and messengers, the characters enable me to pursue an understanding of the mythical history of Wales as part of Western Christian culture and through my imagination articulate my time and place in relation to the past. Myth is often presented as not true, but if we take

Llateies / Y Ddawns – Messenger / The Dance
– *olew ar gynfas / oil on canvas 52 x 41 cm*

myth as being a narrative involving the imagination and embodying popular ideas to explain the existence of a social structure, traditional rites and customs, myth can be seen not as fiction but as a timeless truth repeated over and over again and adapted to suit the particular time and culture. Since ancient times people have remodelled old myths to explain contemporary society; they contain powerful symbols that suggest ways of interpreting and finding meaning in our existence. By understanding these mythical connections, through our imagination, I believe we can realise a greater unity with other people and the natural world.

How women were represented visually continued to be in the forefront of my thinking in 1989 when I began working on ideas for *Bywyd Arall / Another Life*. Throughout the whole time I was making these paintings and drawings, I looked at the way women had been portrayed visually within pre-Christian and Christian mythology. Some of the first paintings I called *Merched y Cwm / Valley Girls*. These are three large canvases based on the images of the Triple Goddess figures usually associated with fertility and common throughout world mythologies. Other female figures began to emerge in these paintings,

Merched y Cwm 1 / Valley Girls 1
– *olew ar gynfas / oil on canvas*
183 x 122 cm

Merched y Cwm 2 / Valley Girls 2
– *olew ar gynfas / oil on canvas*
183 x 122 cm

Merched y Cwm 3 / Valley Girls 3
– *olew ar gynfas / oil on canvas*
183 x 122 cm

Llais / Mân Sôn – Voice / Murmur – *olew ar gynfas / oil on canvas* *183 x 122 cm*

such as the Sheela-na-gig carvings, sometimes found over entrance doors and windows of churches, cathedrals and castles. These are figurative depictions of naked women displaying an exaggerated vulva; there are various interpretations of these figures which include references to the pre-Christian earth goddess and a warning against the sin of lust. Many of the Sheela-na-gig carvings in Britain have been destroyed but recently the figure has become a symbol, empowering women to be unapologetic about the display of their sexuality and to convey the message that we, as women, need to be in control of how our bodies and sexuality are portrayed. It has become an image of rebellion against misogyny rather than an endorsement of it. *Merched y Cwm 1 / Valley Girls 1* is overtly sexual and reflects the Sheela-na-gig; *Merched y Cwm 2 / Valley Girls 2* becomes Modron the Mother Goddess and is based on Gladys and Ceini from Merthyr, and *Merched y Cwm 3 / Valley Girls 3* celebrates women within the burlesque clubbing culture of the South Wales Valleys. The three characters are unapologetic about their sexuality and are empowered to be true to their nature. I wanted to celebrate the many women who had come through very hard times but still retained a youthful spirit.

I am fascinated with stories in Welsh mythology that occur where light and dark exist at the same time and when opposites coalesce, life and death, creation and destruction, inner and outer, presence and absence, microcosm and macrocosm and where people shape-shift; these have become part of my *other world*. In parallel to my existential life, creating characters and worlds for them to inhabit using visual signs, symbols and colour was another way of exploring, through my imagination, aspects of my childhood where my spiritual and psychological journey had begun. The arches of the viaduct that traversed the valley in Pont-y-Moel, where as children we became other people through our imaginations, became the symbol of portals into the other world as well as a bridge that connects one area of the painting to another. Other influences on my painting from my childhood were highlighted when it was pointed out to me that the way I painted reflected Pont-y-pool Japan Ware, which was decorated by covering the object made of tin with a dark lacquer and then decorating it with stronger and brighter coloured designs. These objects gave people in Pont-y-pool a great sense of pride, especially with my

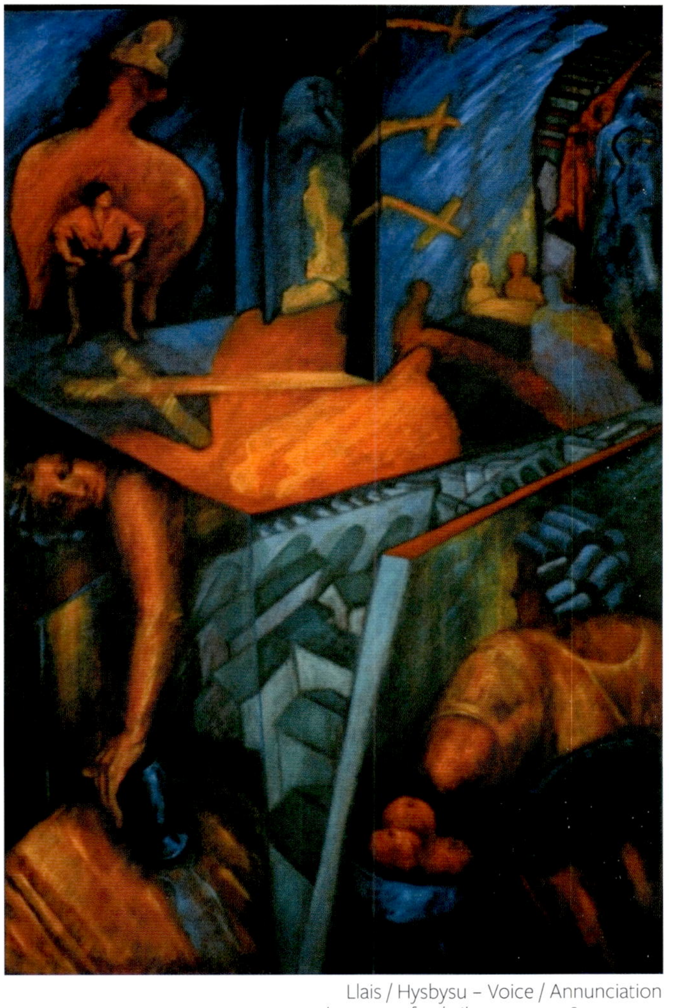

Llais / Hysbysu – Voice / Annunciation
– olew ar gynfas / oil on canvas 183 x 122 cm

family members because a cousin of my grandmother became an expert in the history of the manufacturing process. I had been shown pictures of Pont-y-pool Japan Ware as a child and my grandmother's cousin was talked about often; it did seem a possibility that I had carried these images in my memory which ultimately emerged in my method of painting.

Between 1992 and 1997 I co-founded, organised and taught a course in creative development which was held in a very large farmhouse near the small village of San Sano in the Tuscan hills north of Siena. The course was for people who were interested in developing their creative skills outside their normal working practice. It was very successful, attracting people from Europe and as far afield as Puerto Rico and Russia. The group visited galleries and churches in Siena, where I gave talks about frescoes, stained glass and paintings. For many years I had been interested in the work of Sienese artists between the thirteenth and fifteenth centuries, such as Guido di Sienna, Duccio di Boninsegna, Simone Martini, Pietro and Ambrogio Lorenzetti and Stefano di Giovanni, known as Sassetta. During these visits I became fascinated with the storytelling in some of the paintings, based on a single character which often showed aspects of the subject's life in the surrounding arched niches, as well as the symbolic colour and compositional design. The paintings of the Annunciation intrigued me, in particular the way artists portrayed the relationship between the Angel Gabriel and the Virgin Mary.

In the majority of these paintings the angel is on the left and Mary is on the right but the *gap* between them is always different. What continues to interest me about the *gap* between the angel and Mary in these paintings is because it is where the artist had a choice of what *he* depicted – all the paintings I looked at were created by male artists. The more I looked at the paintings, the more I wanted to offer an alternative interpretation of the way women were portrayed, especially in the story of the Annunciation. The Virgin Mary is often shown as being distracted from a book when the angel tells her she will become miraculously pregnant and give birth to the son of God but will remain a virgin; God is usually represented as an old white man with grey hair and beard. In most of these mythical images Mary submits to the news, with a passive compliance whose fate is dictated by men. There are a few exceptions, such as Sandro Botticelli's painting, the *Cestello Annunciation*, completed in 1489, where Mary appears to be pushing away the angel's message, or Lorenzo Lotto's painting, the *Annunciation* 1534-1535, where Mary is crouching in the left-hand corner, and a cat runs across the floor with an arched back and raised tail. The *gap* I had identified in the paintings of the Annunciation became an important symbol and I adopted the concept as a place where my women characters could

Eiliad yn y Ddawns / A Moment in the Dance
– pastel / siarcol / pensil ar bapur – pastel /charcoal / pencil on paper 30 x 20 cm

become the subject of the image rather than the object, in addition to a symbol for the distance between a spiritual and material life.

For centuries women artists lives were controlled by men, they were constricted as to where and what they studied and were systematically excluded from the records of the history of art. They were able to work in their fathers' or husbands' studios but they were not allowed to draw or paint nude models which was the basic training for male artists. During the period of the late Medieval and through the Renaissance, the way women were represented within Christian visual culture was under the control of wealthy patrons and a male-dominated church. The Genesis creation myth was a favourite subject for paintings

Eiliad yn y Ddawns / A Moment in the Dance – *olew ar gynfas / oil on canvas 41 x 31 cm*

in which naked women were often shown as the embodiment of sin; these were used to illustrate religious and morality stories. Over the centuries naked women took on a sexual role in visual images, when nakedness became nudity and women's sexuality made them objects of men's desire; to commission and own a painting of a nude woman was a way of symbolically possessing her, and objectifying women by male artists continued throughout the modernist period. The majority of paintings of allegorical, classical and biblical mythology were made in artists' studios by men for men. I continued to ask: where were the women artists? Although the names of a few women artists in the late Renaissance/Baroque period were known, such as Sofonisba Anguissola, Lavinia Fontana, and Elisabetta Sirani, their paintings and visual interpretation of Christian and other mythological subject matter has mostly been ignored and disregarded.

Artemesia Gentileschi was the exception, but not initially for her extraordinary expert painting skills. She was born in 1593 and became a pupil of her father, Orazio Gentileschi, a successful Baroque painter in Rome. As a teenager she was apprenticed to the artist Agostino Tassi in her father's studio and, at the age of seventeen, she painted the prescient Susanna and the Elders; a year later she was raped by Tassi. She became famous, not in honour of her magnificent paintings but through the rape trial that began in 1612 and the charges her father brought against Tassi, not because he had raped her but due to the fact that he would not marry her, leaving her unsuitable to marry any other man. We know about the trial because of the detailed court records of the time, which show that Artemesia was subjected to humiliation and torture that could have broken her hand, but, with extraordinary courage and determination, she survived to go on to produce extraordinary paintings, including several versions of Judith beheading Holofernes that are equal to any of those by of male artists of the time. Although her paintings were mostly commissioned by male patrons, she was able to show her personal story by using herself as the model in the grand narrative of mythological paintings as well the allegorical self-portraits, all of which have, for me, a very strong contemporary resonance as the first *confessional* works by a woman artist. In 1638 Artemesia joined her father in London when he became court painter to Charles 1 of England but it has taken until 2020 to be able to see her work in a major exhibition in London.

Wedi Canfod Menywod Coll 2 / Lost Woman Found 2 – *olew ar gynfas / oil on canvas 100 x 100 cm*

Recently, many more women artists of the Renaissance and the Baroque period have been recognised in Italy, which is due in the main to Jane Fortune, an American writer, journalist and philanthropist, who in 2005 began to look carefully at some of the damaged and neglected paintings in palaces, churches and museums, identifying 2,000 forgotten paintings by women in Florence alone. To begin the long process of naming and restoring the works of art she set up a Foundation and employed a team of women art restorers. A pertinent question, for me, is how would it have changed the way women are perceived and the way we perceive ourselves if a female imaginative visual interpretation of the mythical Christian stories, which have been so influential on attitudes towards women in Western society, had been available before. That question is, of course, unanswerable, but it does illustrate how important it is to recognise the female/feminist imagination in the visual art of women today in order to address the influence the male imagination had and still has on women's lives.

Poetry has been central to my creativity. For me reading and responding to poetry is not about making an illustration, but experiencing the poem and then allowing the words to seep into my imagination to stimulate personal visual images. Writing notes and poems, which initially I called 'outbursts,' in my drawing book has played a part in the development of my visual language and, working on *Bywyd Arall / Another Life*, it became clearer that my writing was vital to the process. Reflecting on this, my need to write became stronger and I re-read Edvard Munch's writing in Munch: *In His Own Words*, probably written between 1908 1909. In the section *The Mad Poet's Diary* Munch records that when he wrote notes, accompanied by his drawings, he was making a study of the soul and that he used himself as the subject matter. He goes on to write: 'It would therefore be wrong to look upon these notes as confessions.'[1] He cites the philosophic writing of Søren Kierkegaard to explain why he chose to split his work into two parts: the painter and his mad friend the poet. This description became a sounding board for me in order to explore the parallel lives I had created in image and word and to analyse my need to include notes and poems in the development of my visual language. In 1892 Munch met August Strindberg in Berlin and a friendship developed between the men; the first painting Munch produced in Berlin was a portrait of Strindberg; it was also around this time he painted *The Scream*. This connection renewed my fascination that had emerged during my time in Newport College of Art with the work of artists and writers who had been influenced by psychological and philosophical ideas of this period. The synthesis of image and word in my work was also a way of highlighting the need for women's spiritual, social and political voices to be heard, thereby creating a platform where the inequality, oppression and the abuse women had suffered, and are still suffering, would be acknowledged.

1. Poul Erik Tøjner, *Munch In His Own Words* (London: Prestel, 2001), p.183.

Y Kerchief Goch /
The Red Kerchief
– *gouache ar bapur /*
gouache on paper
84.1 x 59.4 cm

Alibis ***The words I speak***

If I speak the words to fill the absence, will it change the present into the future
revealing the unknown that collects in the heart of uncertainty,
will they change the confetti of alibis that veil the picture
portrayed through a marriage of lies that avoids the truth?
still the words won't come – still the truth is hidden
in layers of excuses embedded in the words I speak.

6

Lleisiau Gweledol a Bydoedd Eraill

Visual Voices and Other Worlds

Llais *Voice*

The visual voices of women have mostly been silenced or ignored within the history of Western Christian culture, as a result of the patriarchal interpretation of scripture chosen by male leaders of the Christian church during its formative years. These biblical texts have remained the canonical stories we have been told throughout the Christian era and have been transformed, with a male gender bias, into the paintings, drawings, sculpture and stained glass which for many centuries helped to transmit the Christian story to people, who in the main, could not read or write. These images were mostly commissioned by the church hierarchy, supported by rich patrons, to illustrate how people should think, behave and believe in order to be accepted by the church, society and the state. The accepted Christian creation myth ignored earlier myths that included a creator who was both male and female, as well as the role of the female divine, including Sophia/Wisdom, in the earlier stories of the formation of humankind. The creation myth in Genesis sets the scene: God creates Eve from the rib of Adam; she is named as the woman who gave the fruit of the tree of knowledge to man and, seeing their nakedness, they were ashamed – a particular patriarchal take on women attempting to obtain and share knowledge.

Feminist Liberation Theologian and writer Lisa Isherwood, Professor Emerita at the University of Winchester, has led the way in debunking the myths that have dominated the perception of women in Western Christian society. She offers an alternative to the dualistic interpretation of the Christian story by suggesting there is a need for women to dislodge the fundamental oppressive and violent nature at the core of the Christ symbol. During my time as a Visiting Research Fellow in the Feminist Liberation Theology Art Forum at Winchester University, Lisa introduced me to the writing of women liberation theologians internationally and their exceptional contribution to a fundamental belief in the importance of women's equality at all levels in an adverse religious environment. These include Rosemary Radford Ruether, Mary Daly, Marcella Althaus-Reid and Grace Jantzen, who I had previously read and had become fascinated by her proposal that we need to look beyond the violent images of a dying man on a cross to a symbolic that embodies birth and flourishing, with women at the centre. An aim of Feminist Liberation Theology is to restructure the patriarchal tenet of Western Christian religious dogma by emphasising gender and sexual equality and a bodily connection with the earth and the cosmic whole, which can offer women freedom from 'keeping silent', being kept 'behind the blue line' and many other exegetical constricts of text from a male perspective.

It was becoming apparent to me that my women characters who inhabited *Bywyd Arall / Another Life* needed to develop, in order to reflect my perception of the way women have been represented in Western Christian visual art. The answer to finding this new direction

Ymson 1 / Soliloquy 1 – *olew ar gynfas / oil on canvas 152 x 152 cm*

Ymson 2 / Soliloquy 2 – *olew ar gynfas / oil on canvas 152 x 152 cm*

Ymson 3 / Soliloquy 3 – *olew ar gynfas / oil on canvas 152 x 152 cm*

came from a completely unexpected source. I knew very little about the Baltic countries, other than they were satellite states under the domination of the Soviet Union and the peoples of the three countries – Lithuania, Latvia and Estonia – had been part of a non-violent revolution for over four years to regain their right to speak their own language, celebrate their own culture and be politically independent; I identified their struggle with our own in Wales. The Baltic States' revolution was called the Singing Revolution because thousands of people in each country would gather together, for safety, to defy the law by singing songs and reading poems in their own language. I had seen images of the 1989 'Baltic Way' in which two million people sang traditional songs as they held hands to form a 600 km human chain along the sides of the roads, starting from Vilnius, Lithuania in the south, through Riga, Latvia to Tallinn, Estonia in the north. Independence was declared in Lithuania on 11th March 1990 but was not recognised by most other countries. The non-violent revolution continued and on 13th January 1991 the Soviet Union sent assault troops and armoured tanks into Vilnius to attack the people who had taken over the television tower. The Soviet troops began shooting, expecting everyone to run away but, instead, thousands more came out of their homes and surrounded the tanks; before the attack was over, 14 people who were moving unarmed and peacefully towards the tanks had been killed and 702 people were injured. It was extremely dangerous for contemporary composers, writers and artists in the Baltic States to produce and present work without the approval of a board of Soviet Union censors; consequently, the language and culture of these countries were kept alive through underground movements.

It was against this background the composer John Metcalf, the artistic director of the Vale of Glamorgan Contemporary Music Festival invited composers, musicians and singers from the Baltic States to perform music from their own countries in the 1996 festival. I had been listening to the minimalist music, inspired in part by Gregorian chant, of composer Arvo Pärt from Estonia but was unfamiliar with composers from Latvia or Lithuania and decided to go to the concert in Llandaff Cathedral. The first half of the concert was, for me, a revelation of contemporary music. As the second half of the concert began a Lithuanian folk horn, sounded as if it was *calling* from the transept. I became acutely aware of a heightening of my senses when a large group of women and children dressed in black, appeared out of the side chapel humming and murmuring with individual voices soaring up from the group slowly making its way along the south aisle next to me. As they walked, their feet, covered in soft material, made the sound of shush-shush-shush on

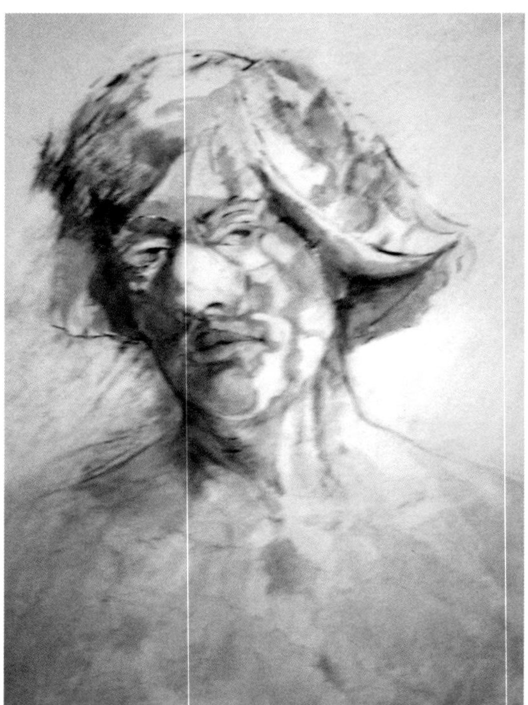

Goeden Afal / The Apple Tree – *siarcol / pensil ar bapur – charcoal / pencil on paper 84.1 x 59.4 cm*

the stone floor. The group encompassed the audience, moving across the rear aisle and down the north aisle like an undulating sound circle. When they reached the transept, their voices became louder. Five women moved out from the front of the group and began singing a haunting repetitive series of words as if they were calling and answering each other; one woman stepped out in front and repeatedly sang an ethereal range of word-sounds that seemed to be suspended in the space above us, taking the music to a higher plane which was harshly blotted out by the massive sound of the Cathedral organ. At that point, I looked at my programme and saw the music was an oratorio called *Last Pagan Rites* by the Lithuanian composer Bronius Kutavičius; I looked up and realised that it was being performed under an arch which supports the figure of Christ in Glory – the *Majestas* by Joseph Epstein.

Throughout this performance I knew I was going through a transformative experience. The connection between a pre-Christian and Christian mythology and how these cultures had influenced the role of women in society formed part of the way my visual language was developing, and hearing this music in these surroundings was the key to stimulating my imagination, giving rise to visual signs and symbols that would appear in my work from then on. The intention of Bronius Kutavičius and the Lithuanian poet Sigitis Geda, who wrote the libretto, was that *Last Pagan Rites*, composed in 1978, should examine symbolically the transition from Paganism to Christianity. The score of the oratorio was written in the form of a circle with precise choreographic directions. Bronius explains 'the children being barefoot in summer or sliding in woollen socks in the winter is significant to the work' adding that 'the loud organ music at the end drowns out paganism'. Bronius and Sigitis Geda said this work, which was extremely daring for its time, celebrated the relationship between humankind, the enduring natural world and the cosmic circle symbolised by the sacred oak tree or the world tree. Like all other new works produced in Lithuania under Soviet rule, this oratorio had, as a matter of course, to be performed in front of the committee of the Composers' Union, which would normally have been a closed, private event. The performance was not advertised, yet many people were aware something highly significant was taking place and, as the news spread, it became both a political and cultural occasion. By now everyone in Lithuania had heard of Bronius Kutavičius and Sigitis Geda and the Baroque Concert Hall in Vilnius was full of people eager to hear the controversial music, which was acclaimed by the audience but didn't receive the approval of the Communist-led Composers' Union. *Last Pagan Rites* was not performed again until 1988, when it became the first music to be played during the reconsecration of Vilnius Cathedral after it had been used as a warehouse during the Soviet era. The oratorio came to be seen by the general public as epitomising the Lithuanian nation and was the precursor of the changes to come.

Ceidwaid y Cofion Ysbrydol / Guardians of a Spiritual Memory 1-6 – *olew ar fwrdd / oil on board 41 x 32 cm*

The characters that had accompanied me in my paintings and drawings for *Bywyd Arall / Another Life* were about to embark on the next stage of my odyssey. Pre-Christian mythological goddess figures together with the Sheela-na-gig continued to play roles, but I wanted to find a way of representing characters from Christian mythology and create a bridge to connect the two. My aim was to create alternative images and symbols to the way women were visually portrayed when the earth goddess became a male god ruling from heaven through the imposition of Christian patriarchy. Initially, these characters were featured in small-scale oil paintings called *Ceidwaid y Cofion Ysbrydol / Guardians of a Spiritual Memory* which I saw as 'stepping stones' enabling the women to move cautiously from one stage to another. I thought of these small images as icons, recalling the symbolism that had interested me during my time in Newport College of Art, in particular the Eastern Orthodox icons which featured the feminine divine in the form of Sophia/Wisdom. Icons are painted to open a portal into another world in order for the viewer to contemplate the divine presence in action and are mostly used for prayerful meditation within Eastern Christian orthodoxy. The modern icon painter is still trained to follow strict rules governed by the subject matter, composition, colour and symbols and is only allowed to copy icons that have been composed and approved by the male Church authorities; I was planning to make images to counterbalance this ethos. The images *Ceidwaid y Cofion Ysbrydol / Guardians of a Spiritual Memory* were a way of endeavouring to convey divine incarnation from a female point of view and were an act of resistance against the domination and control of how we as women have been portrayed. If this is what men think is the imagery that connects us with the divine, what do I think, as a woman, will sustain us in the quest to acknowledge the divine in ourselves and in others, together with the natural world and the universe of which we are a part? What could we learn from the mythologies of the pre-Christian period, which had elevated women as goddesses as part of their story?

Gods and goddesses are figments of our imagination, and patriarchal images of the biblical stories in Christian mythology are the ones most people in Western Christian culture recognise. I thought this was a good place to start to explore how images of women had changed during this transformation. In *Metaphysics as a Guide to Morals*[1] Iris Murdoch writes 'The Judaeo-Christian God owes a considerable debt to art, may even be seen as a work of art.' Women in Western culture, historically, are mostly portrayed in visual language as embodiments of sin or as virgins, mothers, servants, whores and victims, adjuncts under the domination of men's needs. In *Ceidwaid y Cofion Ysbrydol / Guardians of a Spiritual Memory*, the small

Ceidwaid y Cofion Ysbrydol / Guardians of a Spiritual Memory 7 – *olew ar fwrdd / oil on board 41 x 32 cm*

Drawing Book 1-6 – *pastel/pensil ar bapur / pastel / pencil on paper*

paintings, and in the much larger triptych, *Ymson / Soliloquy*, I adopted some of the colour symbolism traditionally used in icon paintings: gold representing the radiance of heaven, red the divine life, blue the colour of human life and white the colour of the uncreated life of God. However, I changed the roles women played in the unfolding drama, enabling them to become the subject not the object of the painting and to own the characters they are playing by being given a visual language voice. In one painting a naked Eve gives and takes the apple, walks over an image of an apple on the floor; her face is painted red, a tribute to the colour of the face, hands and feet of Sophia, representing divine wisdom in Russian icons. In another painting a young girl, not yet awakened by the call of sexual awareness and womanhood, sits and contemplates the apple and in another an older woman meets her younger self and reflects on the past.

The main character in these images personified the female divine; I was looking for a symbol to identify her and decided to use a dark triangular shape to surround her head, which could be read as her hair but more particularly it is a pictorial trope to identify her status in the image. The triangle has become an important symbol in my work, representing the spiritual pathway to enlightenment, revelation and a higher perspective as well as indicating the presence of Sophia/Wisdom. While I was working on these paintings, Osi Rhys Osmond, a constant friend and fellow traveller, who I had met in Newport College of Art in 1960, gave me a book called *The Square Halo & Other Mysteries of Western Art* (1995). The book sets out an analysis of some of the symbols used in Christian religious art, which to my surprise included a triangular halo, incorporated into images depicting the Old and New Testament mythological stories during the fourteenth and fifteenth centuries. I was still unable to understand why this shape had become such an important symbol until I realised one of my favourite photographs taken of my mother in her twenties shows her hair is cut in a 'bob', which forms a triangular shape around her head.

My exhibition of paintings Llais / Voice was exhibited in the Washington Gallery, Penarth in 2000 when *Last Pagan Rites* was being performed for a second time as part of the Vale of Glamorgan Contemporary Music Festival. During this time I met Raminta Lampsatis, the biographer of Bronius Kutavičius, and was invited to Vilnius, Lithuania to exhibit the first series of the *Ceidwaid y Cofion Ysbrydol / Guardians of a Spiritual Memory* paintings in the Opera House, Vilnius when Bronius' opera *Lokys / The Bear* was being premiered. To be exhibiting as part of such an important national Lithuanian occasion was a great honour, and meeting Bronius, his wife, Dalia, and daughter, Ieva, was the

Drawing Book 7 – *pastel / pensil ar bapur / pastel / pencil on paper*

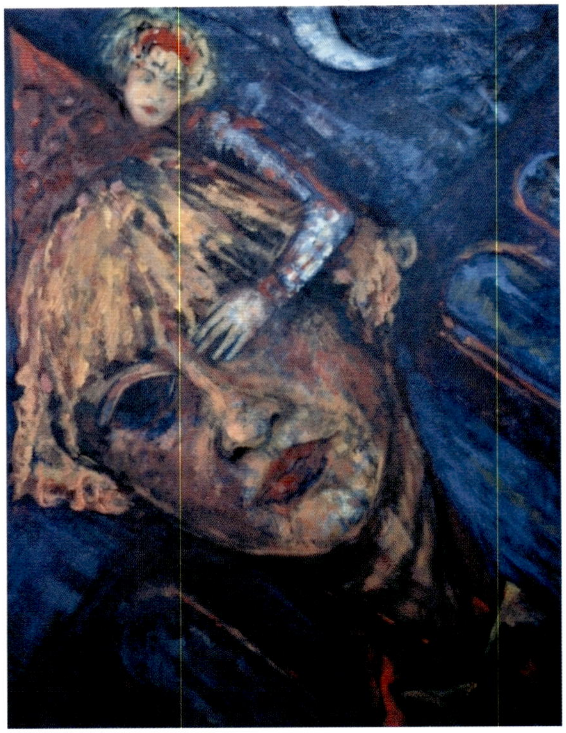

Merch gyda Barcud 2 / Girl with a Kite 2
– olew ar gynfas / oil on canvas 102 x 76 cm

beginning of a friendship and a Wales–Lithuania cultural exchange of poets and artists. My intention has always been to promote the cultural, social and political identity of Wales and to celebrate our unique culture, which is still threatened, and often over-shadowed by England. The question of who speaks for Wales can, in part, be answered by the creative voices from all the arts who speak for Wales.

In the late 1990s I decided to explore the role of drawing and painting in particular to the culture of Wales and it became clear to me the relationship between the word and the image is an important part of our heritage, which was highlighted in the exhibition *META 2000*. I invited eight artists to exhibit and asked each, in turn, to invite a poet whose writing they felt had an affinity with their own work, to partner them in the exhibition where the paintings and poems were displayed together. The first meeting of all the artists and poets was held in 1999 in the Bay Art Gallery in Cardiff where the premise of the exhibition I was planning to initiate, curate and organise was discussed; it became the *META* exhibition and was developed in collaboration with Lynne Crompton, the curator at Oriel Q Gallery in Narberth. This was a gallery Lynne had pioneered and it showed emerging, as well as, established artists; she had built a reputation for the gallery both nationally and internationally and had established important collaborative connections, both cultural and educational, with local communities. My aim in this exhibition was to present paintings and poems that questioned our assumptions about 'reality'. The collaboration between painters and poets was seen as a way of offering an insight into the creative process based on concepts concerned with occurrences firmly rooted in the everyday, but which when mediated through the artist's sensibility and realised through the imagination, culminate in images that engage in the deeper and more meaningful questions about our lives.

In the *META* exhibition it was my intention to show how the role of painting has changed. By looking specifically at the interrelationship between the image and the word we could offer an alternative view, in particular we could acknowledge and celebrate the relationship between the image and the word within the culture of Wales. In the *META* catalogue (2000) author Simon Thirsk wrote:

> While no intelligent artistic interpretation of the contemporary world can ever now be comfortable or uncritical or unaware of itself, it can still contribute to our shared understanding of the imaginative world. These works are deeply self-aware: the artists and poets strive not simply to express themselves, but to image the imagination in a way that is both thinking and knowing. At a meta level, the experience of

Ceidwaid y Cofion Ysbrydol / Guardians of a Spiritual Memory 8-13 – *olew ar fwrdd / oil on board 41 x 32 cm*

Ceidwaid y Cofion Ysbrydol / Guardians of a Spiritual Memory 14-19 – *olew ar fwrdd / oil on board 41 x 32 cm*

Drawing Book 8-13 – *pastel / pensil ar bapur / pastel / pencil on paper*

Drawing Book 14 – *pastel / pensil ar bapur / pastel / pencil on paper*

understanding is itself elusive. It is pushing at the boundaries of our mental capacity to describe how an idea (when we have an impulse to say something, for instance) forms itself into words. How do we describe the experience of that original idea except in words? Thinking about the experience of thinking is thinking at a meta-meta-level. On the surface, visual art appears to be completely independent of words. We look at a painting, or a view or someone's face and it needs no words, we apprehend it in an instant. Below the surface the parallels are surprising: we are not neutral to images; they attract or repel us. [...] Our own act of seeing is always an act of imagination whether the seeing is literal or metaphysical. In examining this act of imagination, we explore the space between art and the apprehension of it.[2]

The *META* exhibition toured from Oriel Q, Narberth to five venues in Wales, and in 2002 it was shown in the Arka Gallery, the principal gallery in Vilnius, founded by the Lithuanian Artists' Association. Some of the artists and poets in *META* travelled to Vilnius for the exhibition preview. While we were there I was told the woman curator of Arka Gallery had been part of the group of 14 people who had walked towards the tanks at the television tower in Vilnius in 1991. She had been holding the hand of a boy who was shot and killed, a stark reminder of the reality of the recent violence. The exhibition formed part of the Poetry Spring Festival held each year in Vilnius and Kaunas, the second-largest city in Lithuania. During a very moving occasion *META* was opened in the Arka Gallery by Welsh and Lithuanian poets reading their work.

Kornelijus Platelis, a poet, translator and essayist, was a wonderful host, he arranged for the artists and poets, who had travelled from Wales to Lithuania for the exhibition, to go to Kaunas for the main events of the Festival. In 2004 he came to Wales, to read his poetry in Chapter Arts Centre and at Oriel Myrddin in Carmarthen. When we arrived in Kaunas, we were given a wonderful welcome by a band playing traditional music and a feast of Lithuanian food and drink. As the ceremony began, I realised that the main event was the crowning of the bard with a wreath of oak leaves, the greatest honour a poet could receive. The similarities between the National Eisteddfod in Wales and this festival in Lithuania were a complete surprise.

In 2003, Menna Elfyn and I were invited to go to the Poetic Fall Festival in Druskininkai. I exhibited my paintings in the Sofa Gallery and Menna read her poetry in Welsh. During this International Festival it was fascinating to hear poetry spoken in

Ceidwaid y Cofion Ysbrydol / Guardians of a Spiritual Memory 20-25 – *olew ar fwrdd / oil on board 41 x 32 cm*

languages from other Baltic and Nordic countries that are in danger of being overwhelmed by English in the digital age. I particularly remember a woman reading her poem in Icelandic and then Menna reading her poetry in Welsh; it was very clear that these festivals were keeping many of the threatened languages alive. During this visit I was introduced to the director of the Nida Artists' Colony, on the Baltic coast, in order to discuss the possibility of developing an artists' exchange programme. Telling him I was from Wales, he looked puzzled, and answered through the translator that he hadn't heard of Wales. I did my usual routine of saying Wales was a country which was part of the British Isles, so he said he would bring a map. The map showed Scotland, Northern Ireland and England but not Wales: it was not named and printed over by the initial 'E' of England, so I found myself attempting to set up an artists' exchange programme with a country which, according to the map, did not exist. I was determined to put Wales 'back on the map' in whatever way I could. This discussion eventually led to an arrangement which enabled Lynne Crompton at Oriel Q to organise a month-long residency in 2004 in the M.K. Čiurlionis Memorial Museum in Druskininkai for two emerging artists, Jesse Brennan and Robert Lawton.

The process of imaging the imagination was at the core of my thinking when I was planning the *META* exhibition. The concept of the initial ideas from artists and poets is based within a common parameter but when mediated through the imagination takes the viewer and reader to a meta level. This was also my starting point when initiating, co-ordinating and developing our book, *Imaging the Imagination: An exploration of the relationship between the image and the word in the art of Wales*,[3] which I co-edited with Ceridwen Lloyd-Morgan. Its aim was to explore this relationship within both a historical and a contemporary context, and it included work by artists whose paintings showed a close affiliation to the word and a connection to the culture of Wales, in particular. The particular relationship between the word and the image in the art of Wales is central to *Imaging the Imagination*. In the first chapter, Ceridwen Lloyd-Morgan illustrates how in early manuscripts the word and the image worked in tandem. The subsequent chapters feature David Jones, Gwen John, Ceri Richards, Brenda Chamberlain and Ernest Zobole, and the final chapter, written by Osi Rhys Osmond, concentrates on contemporary artists. Some of the artists in *Imaging the Imagination* were born in Wales and spent their formative years here, others have made it their adopted home; for some, it has been the inspiration for a lifelong journey of discovery, exploring the diversity of the language and our spiritual, cultural, social and political history. It was my intention that this book would attempt to reach a deeper understanding of the nature of this close relationship between the work of artists who are also writers and artists who have been inspired by writers. This is particularly important and revealing as an aspect of a strong Welsh independent cultural identity from a female perspective.

1. Iris Murdoch, *Metaphysics as a Guide to Morals* (London: Penguin Books, 1993), p.7.
2. Simon Thirsk, META catalogue (Oriel Q, Narberth, 2000), pp.10-11.
3. Christine Kinsey, Ceridwen Lloyd-Morgan (eds.) *Imaging the Imagination: An exploration of the relationship between the image and the word in the art of Wales* (Llandysul: Gwasg Gomer, 2005).

Llateies / Alltud –
Messenger / Exile
– *olew ar gynfas / oil on canvas 152 x 92 cm*

Alibis **The Black Sun**

Negative memories hang in a line of broken images, they emerge
from the inconsolable dark spilling over the boundaries
into shadows that distort the present, without hope of capturing
the past full of hidden dreams, shallow beams of light
fill the frame and constricts the aperture, the future
closing down – closing down until all light is excluded
and the black sun haunts the final scene.

7

Sgyrsiau Mewnol | **Interior Conversations**

Ymddiddan *Colloquy*

CK

Bryan died unexpectedly of cardiac failure in the early hours of 20th October 1997; that terrifying night is a permanent memory. The house and studios we built in Maes-y-crugiau had created an environment where we could support each other as artists and was a home that neither Bryan nor I had experienced before. Over the four years I remained on my own in the house and studio, it slowly became apparent I would not be able to stay in the isolated house and my studio, working as a professional artist and continue teaching in Carmarthen College of Art, where I had taught as a visiting lecturer, with Bryan, for over 15 years. In 2001 I made the heart-breaking decision to move into a rented cottage on the banks of the river Tywi at Nantgaredig and work in a small studio to make a series of paintings and drawings for *Llais / Voice*. After three years I needed to move again in order to find a much larger studio to produce the paintings and drawings I was planning for *Ymddiddan / Colloquy*, which would open in Newport Museum and Art Gallery, Gwent in 2006. It wasn't possible to find an existing affordable space and I made the decision to buy a derelict barn in Treowman, Pembrokeshire with plans to convert it into a studio with living accommodation. Because the conversion took much longer than expected I moved into a caravan on the building site and lived in it for a further year, using a shipping container as a studio.

During this period I lost numerous friends and family; two of Bryan's three brothers died of cardiac failure in Rhymney, Gwent. Bryan and two of his brothers had died of the same disease within eighteen months of each other and I became convinced these deaths were caused, in part, by the poverty they endured as a family when they were growing up during the dismantling of the mining industries and the economic impoverishment it caused in the South Wales Valleys. The tragic death of Bryan's nephew, who had suffered head injuries near his home in Rhymney, was initially treated as a murder case and concluded with an open verdict. The death of my mother at the age of ninety-five in 2003 was an enormous loss but I am so grateful we were able to spend time together during her final years. It was a joy to be in the company of the quiet but resolute and dignified woman she had remained throughout her life. In an attempt to cope with losing the people closest to me I resolved to keep busy.

I continued to produce paintings and drawings and exhibited in South Africa, Lithuania, Spain, Belgium, England, Éire and Wales. I toured *Llais / Voice* to five venues between 2001 and 2005, giving

Teyrnged / Tribute – *olew ar gynfas / oil on canvas 41x 31 cm*

Llateies / Breuddwyd – Messenger / Dream
– *olew ar gynfas / oil on canvas 52 x 41 cm*

'Sun Bathing in the Rain'
– *olew ar gynfas / oil on canvas 66 x 58 cm*

gallery talks and delivering workshops. I curated and organised the META exhibitions, which included poets and painters, in Wales and Lithuania, as well as co-ordinating and editing, with Ceridwen Lloyd-Morgan, the book *Imaging the Imagination – An exploration of the relationship between the image and the word in the art of Wales.* I negotiated with the British Council for our exhibition *Kinsey, Roche, Webster* that consisted of paintings by Catherine Roche, Catrin Webster and myself, which was initially shown Oriel Q, Narberth, to be exhibited in the Centre Cultural, Terrassa, Barcelona. By keeping as busy as possible there was no time to think of the past, but I was often engulfed by uncontrollable waves of grief.

Since 1997 the interior barrier I had built to protect myself from the memories of people I loved and had lost, and whom I hadn't been able to mourn fully, began to crumble until there was no longer a way to avoid facing the grief I had been suppressing for many years. The sorrow and despair became so great it began to affect me physically and mentally; at one of the lowest points, sitting in my studio on a rainy Sunday afternoon feeling emotionally exhausted and not being able to find any energy to work, I began reading Gwyneth Lewis' book *Sunbathing in the Rain*[1] and read it to the end without stopping. The book is about her experience of depression and she describes it as a handbook for fellow sufferers, I recognised what Gwyneth was describing was much of the terror I was feeling by not being able to accept my uncontrollable emotions caused by grief. Reading the moving and reassuring account of her ordeal gave me a reason for hope and a means to try and claw my way back from the edge of an unfathomable void. I believe Gwyneth's book saved me from going into an even darker place because it showed that 'warring' against the overpowering feelings of loss and grief was a sure way of enticing them to take over my mental state and my physical well-being. Nurturing and embracing these feelings gave me the courage to find a creative way of acknowledging and accepting them and begin the process of healing.

In early 2005 I moved, with great expectations, into the converted barn, which I called Pont-yr-Adwy/Bridging the Gap, and my brand new studio. It was the first time I had been still and quiet for more than six years but instead of my creative spirit feeling free and exhilarated about achieving my goal, the whole of my being was overwhelmed by a sense of exhaustion in body and mind. It felt as if I had become two people: there was my body which was empty and another 'me' moving in parallel and knew I would need to find

Yr Adwy / The Gap – *olew ar gynfas / oil on canvas 102 x 77 cm*

Y Ffenestr / The Window – *pensil ar bapur / pencil on paper 84.1 x 59.4 cm*

a way of bridging this divide. It was at this point that my focus changed to constructing more personal characters in my images to help me to connect the two personas I felt I had become. This was very different to the way in which I had consciously created the characters to distance myself from my self in previous paintings and drawings, with whom I had explored my outer and spiritual inner parallel worlds; I knew this feeling of separation was coming from a place deep in my psyche. Somehow these personas needed to be brought together for me to feel whole again. The only way I could change was to draw, paint and write, but now my creativity needed to be from a profoundly personal, psychological source in an attempt to understand what was happening to me physically and mentally.

I had believed being in my new studio would inspire me to start working on the paintings I had planned as the large *Ymddiddan / Colloquy Triptych*; instead, it was impossible to work. On one particular bright, sunlit day, the sun appeared 'black', which had happened on numerous occasions previously but at those times I had found a way of working creatively to change my state of mind. This time it was different. I was in a very dangerous place and knew there were two options: either to be engulfed by a swirling vortex of negativity from which I might not return or to begin to face the emotions created by memories I had been trying so hard to suppress. My emotions had become central to my creativity, therefore my pictorial characters needed to take an alternative path. To begin this interior renewal I incorporated new women characters who would inhabit my paintings and drawings with the purpose of empowering me to re-unite my body and mind and visually connect the separate worlds I perceived my life had become. In the paintings and drawings for the *Ymddiddan / Colloquy* exhibition, I deliberately changed my focus and constructed personal characters from a place deep in my unconscious which entailed finding new symbols that would join the two sides of this emotional divide; consequently, the *gap* as a metaphor in *Llais / Voice* performed another function. I needed to incorporate this symbol as part of the structure of the composition and inhabit the *gap* with a character who would act as a guide. While working on the first large canvas a single standing woman with one bare breast began to emerge out of the darkness that represented the angst of my grief that had caused the depressive state which had engulfed me. To be able to move on I needed to understand who this character was and what narrative was informing these images.

Ymddiddan 1 / Colloquy 1 – *olew ar gynfas / oil on canvas 152 x 152 cm*

Ymddiddan 2 / Colloquy 2 – *olew ar gynfas / oil on canvas 152 x 152 cm*

Ymddiddan 3 / Colloquy 3 – *olew ar gynfas / oil on canvas 152 x 152 cm*

Y Cyfarfod / The Meeting – *olew ar gynfas / oil on canvas 100 x 100 cm*

The mythological storytelling in the *Gnostic Gospels*[2] was a good starting point. I was fascinated by these gospels, which had been discovered in 1945 in caves near Nag Hammadi in the Egyptian desert; it has been estimated by scholars that this library of over 50 ancient gospels had been written in Greek between 120 and 150 CE and translated into Coptic around 350-450 CE by monks in a nearby monastery, who had hidden them in the caves during a period of persecution. The process of verification and the translation of the codices follows a dramatic journey which included individuals and organisations in Cairo, Berlin, Zurich, London and the USA, eventually leading to the translation into English and publication of the mysterious gospels. In her book *The Gnostic Gospels* the scholar Elaine Pagels reveals there is a strong female presence in much of the writing, as in the Gospel of Mary (Magdalene) and in the text Thunder Bronte / Perfect Mind, which is spoken in the voice of a feminine divine power and in the first person singular:

For I am the first and the last.
I am the honoured one and the scorned one.
I am the whore and the holy one.
I am the wife and the virgin...
I am the barren one,
    and many her sons...
I am the silence that is incomprehensible...
I am the utterance of my name.[3]

The Gnostic texts, which include poems, music, dances, rituals, secret gospels, mystical practices and philosophical treatises on the origins of the universe, have been interpreted by some scholars as a psychological exploration of interior self-knowledge, which, for Gnostics, was a key to understanding universal truths. Elaine Pagels' description of how the adepts of Gnosticism advised their followers to develop their spiritual lives resonated with me:

> Like circles of artists today, Gnostics considered original creative invention to be the mark of anyone who becomes spiritually alive ... On this basis, like artists, they express their own insights – their own gnosis – by creating new myths, poems, rituals (...)

Defod / Ritual – *gouache ar bapur / gouache on paper 84.1 x 59.4 cm*

Cymod / Atonement 1-4 – *olew ar gynfas / oil on canvas 40 x 30 cm*

Corff yn Chwilio am Enaid / Body in Search of a Soul – *olew ar gynfas / oil on canvas 72 x 72 cm*

Alibis ***Truth, Lies & Alibis***

Words draw up pale shadows of memory that morph into a palimpsest of thought,
no excuses quell the relentless guilt; I was there but misunderstood the nuances
that deceived the truth, proven guilty by default it's your fault you said from the ache of love
imprisoned in life's rigid pattern stretching out beyond the bonds of youth;
I was not there when you took the chains and uncoupled them from alibis that could
only be sustained by lies.

8

Taith o Ddfod | **A Journey of Becoming**

Gwirionedd, Celwyddau & Alibïau | *Truth, Lies & Alibis*

Y Syrthiad / The Fall – *acrylig ar bapur* /
acrylic on paper 183 x 122 cm

I continued to look for symbols, motifs and visual metaphors to represent my interior life in order for my drawings and paintings to develop, as well as attempting to incorporate stronger and lighter colour, but instead my paintings became darker and darker. While the *Ymddiddan | Colloquy* exhibition was touring between 2006 and 2009 I gave gallery talks, and my experience when it was shown at Oriel Mwldan, Aberteifi was a turning point. The four largest paintings, comprising the *Ymddiddan | Colloquy* triptych and *Disgwyliad | Waiting*, filled the central gallery. They surrounded the viewer, which created an intimate conversation between the viewer and the paintings and the paintings themselves, embodying my intention of creating an *ymddiddan* – a *colloquy*. The figures no longer represented the angst of the depressive state I had experienced when working on the pictures. The life-size figures now symbolised Sophia/Wisdom as a Tywysydd/Guide and Llateies/Messenger merging out of the background, imbuing the images with the inner still and silent space I had searched for within myself, as a result of the very difficult journey I had taken during the time I had been working on the paintings.

I began to think about taking my characters into a different medium, and film seemed the most obvious. To be able to adapt them and my visual worlds into filmic language, I started developing a storyboard with photographs of my paintings and drawings. My plan was for the film to open with church bells ringing and an animated monochrome drawing of The Falling Character representing Sophia/Wisdom, who would become the Tywysydd/Guide, emerging out of the dark and morphing into the first colour image; this sequence would announce that the journey had begun. I would need a woman actor as the Tywysydd/Guide and she would be the main persona performing three roles: The Seated, The Walking and The Standing Characters as she follows a symbolic journey, in real time and in real space, representing women's position in pre-Christian and Christian cultures. The three characters would enact a ritual and each character

Taith 1 / A Journey – *olew ar gynfas / oil on canvas 183 x 122 cm*

Taith 2 / A Journey 2 – *olew ar gynfas / oil on canvas 183 x 122 cm*

would stop to contemplate her particular role at *stations* on the journey; as her role changed so would her clothes and the lighting of the set. The character's movements would be deliberate; she knows where she is going but her actions are slow and thoughtful. I decided my film would be called *Taith / A Journey* and it would be part of my exhibition *Gwirionedd, Celwyddau & Alibïau / Truth, Lies & Alibis*.

To raise money to make the film I applied to the Arts Council of Wales and was delighted when funding was agreed. I had long admired the work of Michele Ryan, who had made films with the women's group Red Flannel Films, as well as Michele's activism in the women's rights movements and much to my delight she agreed to produce my film, with me as director and a performer. Because of Michele's experience and expertise in the film industry she was able to invite highly skilled professional co-workers, John Podpadec as the cinematographer and Sharron Harris as editor, photographer and sound recordist, both of whom made major contributions to the whole process of making *Taith / A Journey*. At our first meeting I showed John Podpadec the storyboard of the photographs of my paintings and drawings, as well as a storyboard with a series of drawings of how my ideas for the film would develop. One of the first things he said to me was 'of course we will be painting with light', which was just what I wanted to hear. My design for the set mirrored the imaginary world in my paintings and was lit in primary and secondary colours; when these were mixed on a neutral background, they produced white, which was a different *light world* to the one I created in my paintings. Colour pigments, when mixed together, produce black, therefore working with light was completely new, surprising and fascinating. In many of my paintings the characters move through time; by portraying them in continuous representation, but filming the characters moving through *actual time*, was a creative space that could expand the story and the way it was being told. Unsure of how projecting the roles of my characters onto a real person would work, I was amazed when Isabella Podpadec, the daughter of the cinematographer, began performing. She was completely immersed in the role of Sophia/Wisdom as the Tywysydd/Guide; Isabella totally convinced me that she became the characters I envisioned. After much musing I decided to play the other character, Llateies/Messenger. In this filmic world we were creating an environment of coloured light, and a real person was playing the roles of my imaginary characters in real time and in real space. It was an entirely different and quite extraordinary experience for me.

To ensure the viewer would be aware that *Taith / A Journey* was located in Wales and was about *Cymreictod*, a sense of feeling/being Welsh, I decided to convey the location by incorporating both poetry and songs in the Welsh and English languages. The poet, musician and singer Lynne Denman worked with me to plan the soundtrack; I had known Lynne for many years and always been very moved by her voice and the essence of her music. Linking words, that were sung and spoken, to each of the storyboard images created the *stations* where the character stopped to perform a ritual on the journey. Working with Sharron, we recorded Lynne's unaccompanied voice to create *vertical* sounds that would link one image with the next. I chose verses from eighteenth- and nineteenth-century Welsh folk poems with texts that evoked birds, the traditional symbols for the characters of Sophia/Wisdom as the Tywysydd/Guide and Llateies as the Messenger. Lynne's poem 'Breuddwyd/Dream' was set to music and my prelude 'In Transit' was spoken. Lynne invited the Estonian musician and singer Sille Ilves to join us; she played an Estonian lyre, which is similar to the Welsh *crwth*, an ancient bowed string instrument, creating a perfect combination of voice and sound. I usually work in silence in my studio, but in this instance, it was an ideal place to have the music and poetry recorded.

It had taken a long time to plan *Taith / A Journey* and in the transitional filmic images, when Sophia/ Wisdom proceeds from the pre-Christian to the Christian mythical location, I finally decided a black and white sequence would be incorporated. As this section

Ffilm – Taith / A Journey – Delweddau Cynhyrchu 1-3 / Production Images 1-3

Ffilm – Taith / A Journey – Delweddau Cynhyrchu 4-9 / Production Images 4-9

developed it became apparent an Isfyd/Underworld was being created in order to connect the two locations. When the Tywysydd/Guide enters the empty black and white world she is in coloured clothes and wearing a red blindfold which disappears as she becomes a dark silhouette and part of this monochrome Isfyd/Underworld. She hears voices murmuring and calling, stops to look back, and sees an older woman Llateies/Messenger approaching. She stops and turns, then walks back and Tywysydd/Guide and Llateies/Messenger meet; their conversation is muffled – my idea was to convey that the older woman is giving a message to the younger woman. They turn away from each other and Llateies/Messenger walks out of view and disappears. The Tywysydd/Guide returns to the world of colour, once again wearing her red blindfold, which she removes and ties around her neck, then continues on her way.

My intention while making the film was to follow the storyboard and the preparations that had been made to explore film as a medium – but I was mistaken. Seeing the whole film for the first time, specifically when Llateies/Messenger meets the Tywysydd/Guide in the black and white transitional section, the sequence represented much more than I could ever have predicted. I realised at this point that many of my paintings and drawings were about searching for a friend, Penny Morgan, who had died, unexpectedly, at the age of twenty-two. Penny was an artist and spent a great deal of time helping us when we were setting up Chapter; because her family home was opposite our house in Cardiff, she lived between the two houses. Penny died in the first year I was on Sint Maarten, where communications were very difficult. The horror of the news of her death was devastating and it felt as if I had been shattered physically and mentally, as there was no opportunity to say goodbye to her. Never having been able to talk about Penny's death, my feelings had been buried. All those years later this film broke through the protective barrier I had built and left me face to face with my memories and emotions.

To try and cope with this revelation I looked for a way to express my feelings creatively and turned to the poetry of Rainer Maria Rilke, in particular *The Sonnets to Orpheus*.[1] These had been written as a memorial to the death of Wera Ouckama Knoop, the daughter of a friend of Rilke, who had died at the age of nineteen. Part of the process of understanding how to assimilate the memories of grief and a way to begin the healing process was to work in my drawing book/journal, writing down each sonnet and responding visually. The black and white sequence in my film shone a spotlight on my past and on many of the childhood memories that had been hidden for so long. I felt overwhelmed by the exposure to these experiences and needed to find a way to assimilate them through my work.

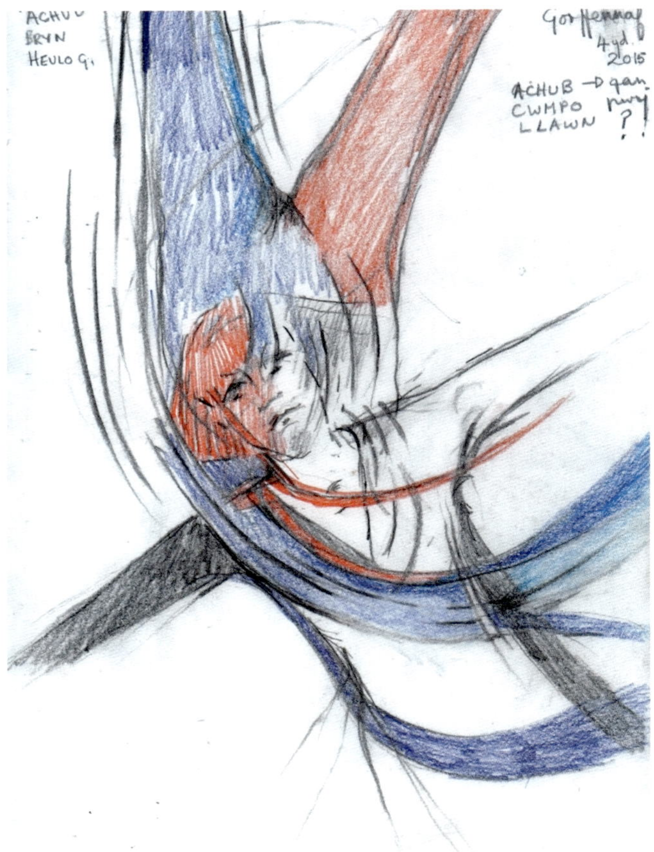

Drawing Book Yr Isfyd / The Underworld 1-2

Drawing Book Yr Isfyd / The Underworld 3-6

Drawing Book Yr Isfyd / The Underworld 7-10

Taith / A Journey – Lluniau Llonydd Ffilm / Film Stills 1-16

To start painting and drawing again was very difficult because I realised I had been running away from what I had been looking for. I was constantly 'talking' my way into an image and then 'talking' my way out again, always attempting to look toward the future. I needed to find the courage to look back and observe my past as I had never done before by striving not to control my visual response, but respond directly in pictorial language to those memories which had been exposed in my film. Looking for meaning and understanding intellectually was the wrong direction and I realised the only alternative was to draw and paint out of my own experience, by allowing images to emerge from my unconscious and engage with my imagination, which is not – as is sometimes described – the ability to invent, but it is the ability to disclose what exists. For this process to be the source of my visual language I needed help and tentatively decided to contact a counsellor who worked through psychosynthesis. This practice has been described as the psychology of the self and acknowledges the realms of human experience, including aspects of the

Drysfa / Labyrinth – *olew ar gynfas / oil on canvas 51 x 41 cm*

Marwnad / Elegy – *olew ar gynfas / oil on canvas 51 x 41 cm*

Myfyrio / Reflect – *dyfrlliw ar bapur / watercolour on paper 84 x 59.4 cm*

soul and spirit alongside physical and emotional experiences, thoughts and mental processes. In the counselling sessions the analysand is encouraged to feel nurtured and strengthened by compassionate attention to the whole of each unique personal identity and encouraged to have a greater connection and understanding of the natural world. After a series of psychosynthesis consultations I felt safe enough to finally acknowledge my deepest memories. Visualisation is an important part of undertaking psychosynthesis and I began the series of what became 36 canvases, each 20 x 20 cm, called *Y Siwrnai / The Journey*. Each painting shows a different memory of growing up in Pont-y-Moel, a place that has been a presence in every image I have produced.

The search for truth – *my truth*, has been the central tenet of my work as an artist; at times it has been very hard to face up to the impact this has had on my life. Visual language is my first language and paintings, drawings and film are where I have had the courage to address being *true to myself*. In attempting to analyse the layers of complexity in our own lives we are able to understand how fluid and transient memory can be. Our identity is often defined by the memories we choose to present as our truth to other people. Sometimes we unconsciously distort memories to cover up the aspects of our lives we don't wish to reveal to ourselves, let alone to others. At significant times memories can open doors into the deepest levels of our being and instigate a way of healing and reconciliation with our past and relationships with other people. One of the most important memories I have needed to try and assimilate was waiting as a child at a bedroom window of our terraced house in Pont-y-Moel, looking out at the Twmp on the lower reaches of Mynydd Maen, and experiencing a column of light moving upwards from the ground, disappearing when it touched the sky, and recognising its powerful presence. The few times I had talked about it the response had been varied: sometimes it was taken to be a Christian religious experience or 'New Age' spirituality, but it is neither of those things. When I first began to try and explain the experience, it was very difficult to describe visually or in words and I have questioned if working as an artist has enabled me to come to a better understanding regarding the essence of the *appearance*; the answer to that question is – I really don't know because I'm still searching for a way to explain the nature of what happened. What I do know is it has been a constant factor in my quest to explore the layers of complexity that make up my life and the world around me. It's an experience I have come to consider as a *glimpse of true reality* and a gift that has taken me in unimaginable directions. Looking back to this time, it is clear to me that what we see and physically experience in our existential lives is not all there is. It has taught me that, as

Tyst / Witness – *olew ar gynfas / oil on canvas 91 x 61 cm*

creative beings, science can show us *what* we are and myths can show us *who* we are. Science and myths are not opposed to each other but are different ways to interpret the world and our place in it. Myths form networks of powerful symbols, which through our imagination suggest particular ways of interpreting the world to give our lives meaning.

Women have been oppressed by the *lies* we have been told by a patriarchal society to silence our voices. This acknowledgement has been critical to the development of my ideas, visual language and creative process. I have dedicated this book to my mother, whose life and work, in the eyes of the British Nylon Spinners factory owners, was worth a fraction of those of the men doing the same job. She was invisible, as were other women who worked in manual industries, this invisibility included women who worked at home supporting their families through extreme poverty. Being invisible still affects the majority of women from working-class backgrounds in the way we are perceived and valued generally and, in most cases, the older we get the more invisible we become. It is still difficult for women to achieve their own expectations within the limitations perpetrated by a male-dominated culture. As a professional artist, I looked for other women nationally and internationally who were like me: from a working-class background and who were promoting women's visibility in order to counterbalance the way we had been portrayed visually for centuries through the male imagination. As I could only find very few named women artists in Western culture, the question *why* continued to dominate my thinking. *Why* was there a lack of visibility for women artists historically and *why* women are still mainly being portrayed by men as objects rather than the subject in most areas of the arts. The question has always been, for me, if the opportunities for women to be artists had been equal to those for men during the past centuries, how would this have changed the status of women and the structures and values in society? Of course, that question can never be answered. Western society is still dominated by dogmatic religious structures and a patriarchal hierarchy and we need to seize the opportunity to visually change the perception of women through the female imagination. Some very brave women in Wales and worldwide are working creatively as political and cultural activists to change the *lies* we are being told. These include how we should look to be accepted, our role in relation to family, how we behave even after suffering physical and sexual abuse, how we are governed and educated to enable us to become financially independent and free to choose – the list is endless. I believe we can change, through the feminist imagination, the way women are being portrayed in all the arts, which will be a positive influence on all our lives. It is by making women the subject not the object in my paintings, drawings and film that I have offered an alternative view. There are very few visual images of Welsh women by women from the South Wales Valleys and my work, including this book, is to see and hear women like myself being given a voice and portraying themselves. When we are not able to see other people like us represented, it is difficult to know who we are and what story to tell ourselves. We can often tell ourselves the wrong story and go along believing it; when it turns out to be the wrong story – we've lived the wrong life.

Writing, particularly poetry/preludes in my drawing book/journal has enabled me to develop my visual language, they have become *alibis* – reasons for not recognising how my paintings and drawings could develop while being overwhelmed by grief and a sense of loss. At these times, when it was difficult to paint, writing was a way of revealing how to creatively open a portal into my visual world. The alibis were crucial in supporting me through very demanding emotional and mentally dangerous times and they continue to be an immediate response to the intensity of my feelings. Although I had included some poems/preludes in the *Ymddiddan / Colloquy* exhibition, I had no intention of including them in this book when was it first planned in 2017; I thought it would be a *visual memoir* and that it

Y N.O.T / The N.O.T – *olew ar gynfas / oil on canvas 91 x 61 cm*

Heddwch / Peace – *olew ar gynfas / oil on canvas 91 x 61 cm*

would not include words. However, I have realised that writing has given me an understanding that I could never have imagined about my identity and place in the world. For this reason I decided to include in this book some *alibis* written over many years, as well as pages from my drawing book/journal to show how my thought process links images to words and how words in turn influence my visual language. Through painting, drawing, film and writing, I have found a way to be in the present more fully and attain reconciliation in my life. In the forefront of my mind has been this wisdom saying from the Gospel of Thomas – a Gnostic text.

> If you bring forth what is within you, what you bring forth
> will save you.
> If you do not bring forth what is within you, what you do
> not bring forth will
> destroy you.[2]

Every painting I have ever made is a fragment of one painting that is still ongoing and the aspects of my life I have recorded in visual and written language, in all the chapters of *Truth, Lies & Alibis*, have influenced my creativity. Writing this book has taught me we are born into our subject matter and the importance of not burying the things that are too distressing to admit or acknowledge to ourselves, let alone to other people. Embracing the difficulties in our lives through creativity can give us the courage to bring all things into the light and respond positively to the freedom this brings.

I have incorporated my beliefs, values and feminist activism into all of my work because, for me, the personal has always been political. I have come to a greater understanding of my role as a woman artist in a male-dominated society by continuing to ask the question : 'If I don't believe what I hear men say, then what do I believe? If I don't think the way men think, then what do I think?' The process includes writing this book, which has been a way of constructing an identity in order not only to understand myself more fully but also to contribute to the well-being of other women. My intention is to fill the gaps in stories told about women who come from the South Wales Valleys. Our stories witness our lives and through creativity we are able to hold a mirror up to human nature as well as the culture in which we live and report it truthfully. We, as women, can learn to tell our own stories through the female imagination. Until this is possible none of us is

Gwylnos / Vigil – *olew ar gynfas / oil on canvas*
91 x 61 cm

truly free to be who we are. Curating and editing *HON: Artistiaid Benywaidd yng Nghymru | Women Artists in Wales 2022* which was published by Ali Anwar the Hm'm Foundation, is a way of providing a platform for women artists from all over Wales to portray, through a personal visual language and their own words, in Welsh and English, a view of their lives and a panoramic view of Wales through the female imagination.

In March 2020, the educational system, economic structure and individual lives in Wales, as across the world, were locked down to prevent the spread of the Covid-19 virus and its variants that have caused the death of over eleven thousand people in Wales and more than 6.7 million people worldwide. We – including schoolchildren – were told to stay at home to work, stay away from people, and wear masks to cover the lower half of our faces, which has given rise to a feeling of isolation from any social or physical contact. The statistics of mental illness caused by the isolation, sometimes in dire circumstances, have yet to been fully assessed but the indication is that there will be a massive increase. The situation has affected everyone in inconceivably different ways and the necessity for us to establish a new world order to enable humanity to survive has been made clear. These new worlds will need to have the well-being of our planet at the centre of the way we live. An area that has played an important role in coping with this very difficult time are the creative arts, which have taken us out of the confines of our homes and deep into our imaginations; these worlds have shown us the importance of the environments that we create for ourselves, and remind us of our creative resilience and capacity for change. Turning to the creative arts has been an affirmative way to keep people connected and to acknowledge the importance of community. We are an integral part of this world and how we live our lives matters to the survival of each other, the natural world and our planet. As an element in the nature of space, I imagine us as part of a finely woven matrix which is in a continuous state of flux and we are irrevocably caught up in its rhythm from our birth to our death.

Bearing witness to the way women continue to experience psychological, physical and sexual exploitation all over the world has provoked my quest to highlight and attempt to change the situation. The development of my women characters and creating worlds for them to inhabit has been an important part of my need to attempt to understand and visualise living at this time. In many areas of creativity women have often been overlooked or, if represented at all, we are included as an adjunct to the main topic. My aim is to share my experience in the hope of connecting with other women and creating a way for us all to have our voices heard. By making our lives visible through our imaginations we can tell our own stories, which are unique and a precious part of a *journey of becoming* in an unfolding universal story.

1 *Rilke's Late Poetry:* (G. Good, Trans,). (Vancouver: Ronsdale Press, 2004).
2 Elaine Pagels, *Beyond Belief: The Secret Gospel of Thomas* (London: Pan Macmillan, 2005), p.32.

Dwyn Tystiolaeth / Bearing Witness – *olew ar gynfas / oil on canvas 183 x 122 cm*

Cydnabyddiaeth | Commentaries

Osi Rhys Osmond *- Taith y Pererin wrth Baentio a Darlunio / A Pilgrim's Progress in Painting and Drawing - Catalogue*

The still small voice may reveal great truths just as shouts and tumults may signify nothing. In an age when bigness, novelty and amplification are the touchstone of art, the work of Christine Kinsey brings an intense poetic vision to pictures so unique, so authentic as to make the viewer feel as an intruder into the artist's own mysterious world. Outside our conception of time, St Augustine spoke of 'three times; a present of things past, a present of things present and a present of things future'. The human imagination can travel in any direction in time and space while we ourselves are propelled relentlessly forward by our destiny. 'The moment of vision' which motivates and triggers the artist's response, is able in certain people to reappear and returns to the consciousness throughout our waking and sleeping hours. Christine's work deals with what Wordsworth called 'rememberable things', she paints in a traditional way with gouache on paper, she embodies an understanding beyond reality. Alongside the lingering recollection of childhood in Wales, she articulates the emotion of the biblical women and connects these to the Pilgrim's Progress witnessed in the cultural dislocation of the West Indies. This work is a journey, it is also a vessel; the journey is physical and spiritual, concerned with the passage of time, place and person. The journey and the vision is encapsulated into a moment, the moment is here.

Gilly Adams *- Cymreictod - Menywod Cymru / Women of Wales catalogue*

So much discussion about 'Cymreictod', about being Welsh, is conducted as though Welshness is an absolute quality which can be set down upon the tablets rather than something which is made up of many different elements, something which we experience and acknowledge more easily than we can define. Christine Kinsey's exhibition reflects one woman's attempts to examine her own consciousness of feeling Welsh – rather than British – an attempt to name herself, her roots, her place in the world and to say something about their meaning in her life. Perhaps also to ask why? To try to find out what sense of place, of history, of belonging imbues us with the sense that this, rather than any other, is our place in the world. There is something very moving about this collection of portraits – this record of so many different lives and relationships across the generations. Each face bears witness, carries the imprint of the particular life experience. The special shock of this exhibition is that the faces which command our attention are women's faces. We have so little access to information about the lives of our mothers and grandmothers, lives which have so often been submerged by the patriarchal view of history. These paintings help to make Her story visible and in doing so celebrate the value of the ordinary, which is so often unsung. Indeed, if you look properly at these portraits you can see how the ordinary becomes extra ordinary in the strength and stamina which has allowed so many of these women to triumph over the hardships of their everyday lives. It is to be hoped that one of the effects of this powerful exhibition will be to draw attention to the paintings by and about Welsh women which exist in the National collection and which do not get the prominence which they deserve – not to mention the portraits of women which must be hidden away in girls' schools and similar institutions throughout Wales. [...] In this exhibition, the lives and passions, sacrifices and joys of these other Welsh women are reclaimed from invisibility and celebrated as a testimony for their posterity and for their own 'Cymreictod'.

Alan Osborne - *Bywyd Arall / Another Life - catalogue*

I came from a mountain place where stones were given names, remains of old iron works became places from another planet, and certain rock formations in the hills were said to have a meaning beyond our understanding. The place was built on fire, parts of the woods had their own mythology and even particular trees were witness to strange events. There were hundreds of these images and stories and I went to Newport Art College with a collection of such fertile imaginings; I met Christine Kinsey there. I believe that artists try to stimulate more perceptive thinking by gently shifting our way of seeing. In this present exhibition, Christine has focussed on the images of women, and has again made me feel aware of the history beneath. This new unification encourages a view which breaks with the traditional images of women, and Wales. The individual pieces are powerful and poignant and give out a spirit and imagination which transcend our perception of reality and instil an experience of a disciplined rapture. Through the progression of these pieces she shows us that a quest for individual salvation can move toward a universal solution. This new work is spiritually and intellectually in the forefront of artistic development in this country. From the very unity of metaphor, symbol, colour and design in these powerful works spring the essential truths of Christine Kinsey's concerns as an artist. These invocations share with us insights into the overwhelming complexity of the human condition.

Ivor Davies - *Bywyd Arall / Another Life - catalogue*

Christine Kinsey has described her paintings and drawings in this exhibitions as being concerned with 'knowing about' growing up female and the feeling of being Welsh. There may be something autobiographical in all painting, but here the emblems, symbols and stories of her life are deliberately enshrined in the characters who enact various parts of her formative years in the Gwent valleys. Even because of her intensely personal attachment to a particular locality, universal values applicable to all humanity are disclosed. They are not portraits, but different characteristics of herself or the female self, either in isolation, superimposed, or like the Janus of European antiquity and as Celtic counterparts. Metamorphosis and the embodiment of more than one modality of the same person, either overlapping or at different moments has also been recorded in former ages: Hekate, the deity connected with magic and spells, presided over crossroads. Here statues were erected to her in the form of a woman with three bodies.

Furthermore, ancient representations of the ages of woman provided a subject for artists at least five hundred years before the symbolism of Munch... It is interesting to see the preparatory drawings. They are precisely studied and transposed into paintings. Art as the imitation of nature or as pictorial decoration is valuable. However, Christine Kinsey conveys ideas directly and without affectation, seeking to reveal and to be herself in a personal and original way, while she draws from her life and soul.

Francesca Rhydderch *- Llais / Voice - catalogue*

I drove out to visit Christine Kinsey in Maes-y-crugiau while she was putting the finishing touches to her paintings for this exhibition. It had been a stiflingly hot summer's day and, even now, in the late evening, the air was still. Passing through high-hedged lanes I caught sight of enormous bales of hay in the fields to either side. As dusk fell they took on a forbidding aspect, wispy glinting sentinels who guarded the gateway to another world. My memory of that drive later seemed curiously appropriate, as when I stepped into Christine Kinsey's studio, the shapes, forms and colours that greeted me in the fading light did indeed seem to have come from another world. Or rather from another existence, from another plane of perceived reality. In a postmodern era in which the deeper meaning of art is increasingly rubbished in favour of Saatchi-style ephemeral novelty, I still cling to a belief in the transcendental power of art, of a poem, of a painting, of a piece of music. As Christine Kinsey herself has said of the process of creating a work of art: 'Finally something says, "this is real!" Then I stop – I feel whole'... Such is the scope of Christine Kinsey's ambition, and such is the humbling, inspiring nature of her success.

Ann Oosthuizen *- Ymddiddan / Colloquy - A commentary on the painting Corff yn Chwilio am Enaid / A Body in Search of a Soul*

A visionary, Christine Kinsey moves as a protagonist through her own paintings searching for a way through the dualities that confront her past/present, mother/daughter, male/female, inner/outer, death/life, creative/spiritual. Her paintings journey to metamorphosis and transformation. The painting I have chosen is a large oil which Christine has called *Corff yn Chwilio am Enaid /A Body in Search of a Soul.* The woman who stares out at us seems to be experiencing tremendous sorrow or grief. Behind her several female figures are silhouetted in curtains of light. Are they people she has lost? Or are they versions of herself, possibilities, choices? In her grief at the death of her closest companion as well as the death of her mother, Christine found comfort and inspiration in writing as well as reading poetry. *The Sonnets to Orpheus* by Rainer Maria Rilke (Vancouver: Ronsdale Press, 2011). were the starting point for a series of images in her drawing book and paintings... I have chosen this picture because I think it demonstrates her steady determination, even optimism, in her search for an identity in an uncertain universe.

Special thanks to:
Hilary Rhys Osmond for her constant friendship and our inspiring conversations while creating this book.

Acknowledgements and thanks to:
Publisher – Ali Anwar the H'mm Foundation, Designer – Andy Dark

Menna Elfyn, M. Wynn Thomas, Alison Webster, Gilly Adams, Heike Roms, Mike Pearson, Geoff Moore, Peter Mumford, Michael Molloy, Hannah Firth and the Team at Chapter Arts Centre, Cardiff

National Library of Wales Archive Centre Aberystwyth; Express Imaging Cardiff; Gwasg Gomer Press for their support since my first catalogue in 1989.

All photographs are by Christine Kinsey, Bryan Jones, Mik Flood unless otherwise specified.

TAITH / A JOURNEY – Film Credits: Producer – Michele Ryan / Director – Christine Kinsey / Cinematographer – John Podpadec / Editor, Photography, Sound – Sharron Harris / Performers – Isabella Podpadec and Christine Kinsey / Composer, Voice – Lynne Denman Musician, Voice – Sille Ilves; Documentary film – Sharron Harris.
Taith / A Journey is dedicated to Penny Morgan 1954-1977

Note page 199 – This painting is a homage to the Lebanese women activists, ABAAD, Artist – Mireille Honein and the campaign 'A White Dress Doesn't Cover Rape'

Alibis from my Drawing book
Chapter 1 / Looking both ways – Chapter 2 / In transit – Chapter 3 / Crossing Borders –
Chapter 4 / Aberfan Disaster 9-15 a.m. Friday 21st October 1966 – Chapter 5 / The Red Kerchief
Chapter 6 / The words I speak – Chapter 7 / The Black Sun – Chapter 8 / Truth, Lies & Alibis.

Other books:
Imaging the Imagination – A Exploration of the Relationship between the Word and the Image in the Art of Wales – Foreword: M. Wynn Thomas, Editors: Christine Kinsey and Ceridwen Lloyd – Morgan; Published by Gwasg Gomer Press, Llandysul, Ceredigion 2005

HON Artistiaid, Benywaidd yng Nghymru – Women Artists in Wales Editor: Christine Kinsey; Published by Ali Anwar the H'mm Foundation, 2022

Christine Kinsey

Selected C.V.

Christine Kinsey was Co-Founder and Artistic Director of Chapter Arts Centre, Cardiff, Co-founder of Artists and Designers in Wales Association, Artistic Advisor to Cardiff City Council on the re-development of Cardiff City Centre. She has had six national and four international solo touring exhibitions, and has exhibited and has paintings in collections in Belgium, Caribbean, Catalonia, Eire, England, Lithuania, Scotland, Switzerland, U.S.A. Wales. Her work is represented in the Victoria and Albert Museum, London; National Library of Wales, Aberystwyth; Glyn Vivian Art Gallery and Museum, Swansea; Contemporary Art Society of Wales collection, National Museum of Wales, Cardiff; Newport Museum and Art Gallery, Newport, Gwent. She has been an Honorary Research Fellow in the Faculty of Art and Design, Swansea Metropolitan University, Wales and Visiting Research Fellow in the Institute of Theological Partnerships, Winchester University, Winchester, England and was awarded The Arts Council of Wales' Mainline Production and Development Grant 2010 / 2011. During 2012 / 14 to celebrate the Centenary of R.S. Thomas she curated and organised the festival and exhibition Correspondences: Contemporary painting in response to the life and writing of R.S. Thomas which was commissioned and hosted by Oriel Plas Glyn-y-Weddw, Llanbedrog, Gwynedd.

Other publications from the H'mm Foundation

Encounters with Nigel Jenkins
Edited by Jon Gower

CONTRIBUTORS:
Edwina Hart AM, John Barnie, Stevie Davies, Steve Griffiths, Angharad Jenkins and Branwen Jenkins, Noel Witts, Deborah Llewelyn, Robert Minhinnick, Peter Finch, John Davies, Menna Elfyn, Delyth Jenkins, Daniel G. Williams, Dave Hughes, Margo Morgan, Janet Dube, Jane James, Steve Griffiths, Ivor McGregor, Benjamin Palmer, Dave Oprava, Iwan Bala and Twm Morys, Janice Moore Fuller, Mike Parker and Ceri Wyn Jones, Ifor Thomas, Jane Fraser, Martyn Jenkins, Carey Knox, Steve Dube, Humberto Gatica, Tom Jenkins, D.J. Britton, Fflur Dafydd, Anne Lauppe-Dunbar, M. Wynn Thomas, Jon Gower and Peter Gruffydd.

ISBN 978-0-9927560-4-8

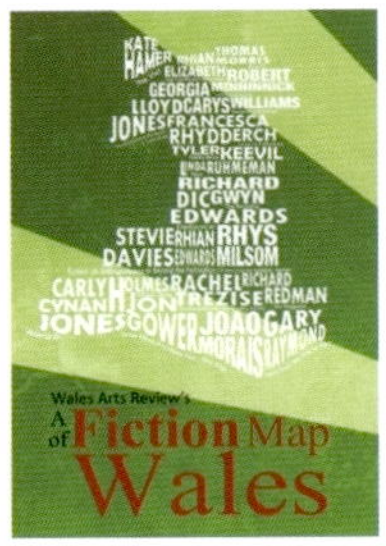

A Fiction Map of Wales
Edited by John Lavin

CONTRIBUTORS:
Rachel Trezise, Thomas Morris, Stevie Davies, Cynan Jones, Francesca Rhydderch, Joao Morais, Jon Gower, Rhian Elizabeth, Carly Holmes, Lloyd Jones, Gary Raymond, Tyler Keevil, Richard Redman, Georgia Carys Williams, Rhian Edwards, Rhys Milsom, Dic Edwards, Linda Ruhmeman, Richard Gwyn, Kate Hamer and Robert Minhinnick.

ISBN 978-0-9927560-6-2

Encounters with R.S. Thomas
Edited by John Barnie

CONTRIBUTORS:
Gillian Clarke, Fflur Dafydd, Grahame Davies, Gwyneth Lewis, Peter Finch, Jon Gower, Menna Elfyn, Osi Rhys Osmond, Jeff Towns, Archbishop of Wales Barry Morgan, M. Wynn Thomas and First Minister of Scotland Alex Salmond.

ISBN 978-0-9927560-0-0

Encounters with Dylan Thomas
Edited by Jon Gower

CONTRIBUTORS:
Rachel Trezise, Michael Bogdanov, Kaite O'Reilly, D.J. Britton, Dafydd Elis-Thomas AM, Dai George, Sarah Gridley, Sarah King, Jeff Towns, George Tremlett, Steve Groves, Gary Raymond, Guy Masterson, Jon Gower, Horatio Clare and Andrew Lycett.

ISBN 978-0-9927560-2-4

It is as if... fragments
Essays about recent work by Iwan Bala, with images and DVD of the PROsiect hAlcw performances in collaboration with musician Angharad Jenkins, based on the poetry of her father, the late Nigel Jenkins.

CONTRIBUTORS:
Iwan Bala, Dr Anne Price-Owen, Osi Rhys Osmond, Twm Morys, Aneirin Karadog and Angharad Jenkins.

ISBN 978-0-9927560-8-6

Encounters with Osi
Essays about Osi Rhys Osmond, edited by Iwan Bala and Hilary Rhys Osmond.

CONTRIBUTORS:
Iwan Bala, Hilary Rhys Osmond, Ivor Davies, David Alston, M. Wynn Thomas, John Osmond, Christine Kinsey, Dai Smith, Karl Francis, Wyn Morris, David Parfitt, Mick and Thea Arnold, Hedley Jones, Noelle Francis, Susanne Schüeli, Teilo Trimble, Bella Kerr, Steve Wilson, Sam Vicary, Tina Carr, Siân Lewis, Nathan Osmond, Sara Rhys-Martin, Luke Osmond, Simon Thirsk, Lynne Crompton, Gwenan Rhys Price, Linda Sonntag, Rolf Jucker, Ché Osmond, Macsen Osmond, Colin Brewster, Ben Dressel, Megan Crofton, Lesley Davies, Beverley Oosthuizen-Jones, John Barnie, Menna Elfyn, Richard Pawelko and Mary Simmonds, Bethan John, Mererid Hopwood, Ann Oosthuizen,

ISBN 978-0-9927560-9-3

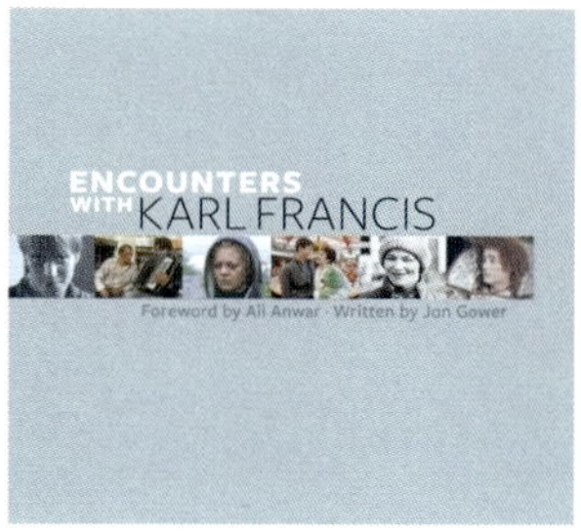

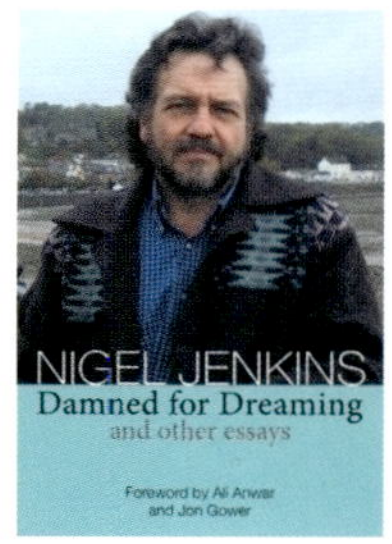

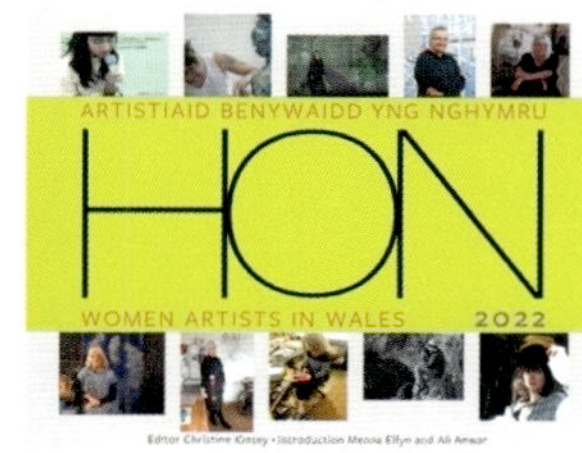

Encounters with John Selway
By Jon Gower

CONTRIBUTORS:
Paul Bowen, Derek Butler, Ivor Davies, Ken Elias, Richard Frame, Karl Francis, Brian Gardiner, Jonathan Glasbrook-Griffiths, Robert Alwyn Hughes, Alison Howard, David Hurn, Julian Meek, Phil Muirden, Osi Rhys Osmond, Brian Rice, Dai Smith, Marion Sprackling, Norman Toynton, Keith Underwood, Peter Wakelin, Phil Watkins, Roger and Den Wolfe.

ISBN 978-1-9999522-0-4

Encounters with Karl Francis

CONTRIBUTORS:
Foreword by Ali Anwar, written by Jon Gower

ISBN 978-1-9999522-1-1

Nigel Jenkins
Damned for Dreaming and other essays

CONTRIBUTORS:
Foreword by Ali Anwar and Jon Gower

ISBN 978-1-9999522-8-0

Osi Rhys Osmond
Cultural Alzheimers and other essays

CONTRIBUTORS:
Foreword by M. Wynn Thomas and Ali Anwar

ISBN 978-1-9999522-9-7

HON
Artistiaid Benywaidd Yng Nghymru / Women Artists In Wales 2022

CONTRIBUTORS:
Foreword by M. Wynn Thomas and Ali Anwar

Introduction by Menna Elfyn

Artists:
Marian Delyth,
Sadia Pineda Hameed,
Angharad Pearce Jones,
Julia Griffiths Jones,
Christine Kinsey,
Sian Parri,
Sarah Rhys,
Catrin Webster,
Sarah Williams,
Sarah Younan.

ISBN 978-1-9999522-6-6

Wicked Words
£2.95

In partnership with The Wales Millenium Centre in 2015

ISBN 978-0-9927560-7-9

H'MM
10th ANNIVERSARY

The H'mm Foundation, Grove Extension, Room 426,
Swansea University, Singleton Park, SA2 8PP.
info@thehmmfoundation.co.uk
www.thehmmfoundation.co.uk